THE *Joy* OF *Christmas*

THE *Joy* OF *Christmas*

EDITED BY KELLY RILEY BAUGH

Guideposts.

NASHVILLE, TENNESSEE

ISBN 0-8249-5897-7

Published by Ideals Publications
A division of Guideposts
535 Metroplex Drive, Suite 250
Nashville, Tennessee 37211
www.idealsbooks.com

Publisher, Patricia A. Pingry
Book Editor, Kelly Riley Baugh
Art Director, Eve DeGrie
Designer, Georgina Chidlow-Rucker
Permissions Editor, Patsy Jay
Copy Editors, Marie Brown, Melinda Rathjen

Color separations by Precision Color Graphics, Franklin, Wisconsin

Printed and bound in the U.S.A. by RR Donnelley

10 9 8 7 6 5 4 3 2 1

ACKNOWLEDGMENTS

BATCHELOR, MARY. "Papa Panov's Special Christmas" by Leo Tolstoy, retold by Mary Batchelor in *The Lion Christmas Book*. Copyright © 1984. Used by permission of William Neill-Hall Ltd. CAPEK, JINDRA. "A Child Is Born" by Jindra Capek, adapted from an old Christmas legend, trans. by Noel Simon. Copyright © by Bohem Press, Zurich, and used by permission. CHUTE, MARCHETTE. "We have been helping with the cake . . ." from *Rhymes About the Country*. Copyright © 1941 by the Macmillan Co. CROWELL, GRACE NOLL. "Whatever else be lost among the years . . ." from *Poems of Inspiration and Courage*. Copyright © 1928, 1934 by Harper & Row, renewed 1956, 1962 by Grace Noll Crowell. Used by permission of Harper-Collins Publishers. FARJEON, ELEANOR. "Through a Shop Window" from *Come Christmas* by Eleanor Farjeon. Copyright © 1927 by J. B. Lippincott Co. Used by permission of David Higham Assoc. FIELD, RACHEL. "For Christmas" from *The Pointed People* by Rachel Field. Copyright © 1924 by The Yale University Press. "Eighth Street West" from *Branches Green* by Rachel Field. Copyright © 1934 by Macmillan Publishing Co., renewed © 1962 by Arthur S. Pederson. Used by permission of Simon & Schuster Children's Publishing Division. FISHER, EILEEN. "Christmas Shoppers." Copyright © by Aileen Fisher. Used by permission of Marian Reiner, Literary Agent. FROST, FRANCES. "To a Christmas Tree" from *The Little Whistler* by Frances Frost. Copyright © 1949 by McGraw-Hill Inc. GRAHAM, BILLY. A quote from *Day By Day With Billy Graham*. Used by permission of The Billy Graham Evangelistic Assoc. GRAHAM, RUTH BELL and GIGI GRAHAM TCHIVIDJIAN. "Christmas at Our House" from *A Woman's Quest for Serenity*. Copyright © 1981 by Gigi Tchividjian. Used by permission of Gigi Graham Tchividjian. HUGHES, LANGSTON. "Carol of the Brown King" from *The Collected Poems of Langston Hughes*. Copyright © 1994 by The Estate of Langston Hughes. Used by permission of Alfred A. Knopf, a division of Random House, Inc and Harold Ober Assoc. JAY LIVINGSTON and RAY EVANS. "Silver Bells." Copyright © 1950. Used by permission of Hal Leonard Corporation. MCGINLEY, PHYLLIS. "All the Days Of Christmas" from *Merry Christmas, Happy New Year*. Copyright © 1958 by by Phyllis McGinley, published by Viking Press. Used by permission of Curtis Brown, Ltd. NORRIS, LESLIE. "The Shepherd's Dog" from *Norris Ark*. The Wells College Press. Used by permission of the author. RICHARDSON, ISLA PASCHAL. "Christmas Shopping" from *My Heart Waketh*. Branden Publishing Company. Used by permission of the publisher. SHAW, ISABEL. "Christmas Chant." From *Jack and Jill*. Copyright © 1949 by Children's Better Health Institute, Benjamin Franklin Literary & Medical Society, Inc. Used by permission. SHELDON, LURANA. "If you've lost your zest for Christmas, . . ." from "Something Wrong." First appeared in *The New York Times*, and used here with "no objection." STROCK, CLANCY. "The Best Tree Ever" from *The Christmases We Used to Know*, edited by Mike Beno. Copyright © 1996 by Reminisce Books and Magazine, and used here with permission. THOMPSON, DOROTHY BROWN. "Christmas Eve" from *A New Christmas Treasury*. Copyright © 1954 by Dorothy Brown Thompson. "Good Will to Men: Christmas Greetings in Six Languages." Copyright © 1933 by Dorothy Brown Thompson. Both selections used by permission of McIntosh and Otis, Inc. TIPPETT, JAMES. "Do Not Open until Christmas: and "Counting the Days" from *Counting the Days* by James Tippett. Copyright © 1940 by Harper & Bros. VAUGHN, BILL. "Tell me a Story of Christmas" Copyright © 2005 by *The Kansas City Star*. Used by permission, not an endorsement. Selections by Idella Bodie, Dina Donahue, and Marjorie Holmes under copyright © by Guideposts, NY. Our sincere thanks to those authors or heirs who submitted original material for use by Ideals Publications.

All possible care has been taken to fully acknowledge the ownership and use of selections in this book. If any mistakes or omissions have occurred, they will be corrected in subsequent editions, provided notification is sent to the publisher.

PHOTOGRAPHY CREDITS

Cover, VCL/Spencer Rowell/Getty Images; pages 6–7, 116–117, 138, 143, 146, William H. Johnson; pages 9, 77, 82, 126–127, 152, Larry Lefever/Grant Heilman Photography, Inc.; page 12, Shaffer/Smith/SuperStock; pages 14, 18–19, 32, 39, 40, 44, 62, 64, 98, 100, 120, 122, Jessie Walker; pages 16–17, 22, D. Petku/H. Armstrong Roberts; page 24, Bruce Avery/SuperStock; pages 26, 52–53, 106, 110, age fotostock/SuperStock; pages 29, 61, G. Ahrens/H. Armstrong Roberts; pages 30–31, 46, Gary Kreyer/Grant Heilman Photography, Inc.; pages 54–55, 148–149, F. Sieb/H. Armstrong Roberts; pages 56, 104, Dianne Dietrich Leis/Dietrich Photography; page 67, Barry Runk/Grant Heilman Photography, Inc.; pages 74–75, M. Gibson/H. Armstrong Roberts; pages 80, 97, Fred Habegger/Grant Heilman Photography, Inc.; pages 85, 112, H. Armstrong Roberts; page 88, A. Teufen/H. Armstrong Roberts; pages 92–93, Digital Vision Ltd./SuperStock; page 94, Thomas Hovland/Grant Heilman Photography, Inc.; pages 114–115, R. Krubner/H. Armstrong Roberts; page 120, David W. Middleton/SuperStock; page 124, f1 online/Alamy; page 130, imageshop—2efa visual media uk ltd/Alamy; page 133, Dick Dietrich/Dietrich Photography; pages 134–135, 144, Carr Clifton; pages 136–137, E. Cooper/H. Armstrong Roberts; page 155, Isaac Geib/Grant Heilman Photography; page 158, Index Stock/Alamy.

TABLE OF CONTENTS

CHAPTER ONE

The Joy of Decorations

Reds and yellows, blues and greens—
Christmas paints her Yuletide scenes:
Brilliant cards in colors bold,
Ornaments of red and gold,

Festive stores and scenery,
Frosty panes in filigree,
Trees ashine in silvered snow,
Star-strung avenues aglow . . .

—NORA M. BOZEMAN

December

HARRIET F. BLODGETT

Oh! holly branch and mistletoe,
  And Christmas chimes wherever we go,
And stockings pinned up in a row!
  These are thy gifts, December!

And if the year has made thee old,
  And silvered all thy locks of gold,
Thy heart has never been a-cold
  Or known a fading ember.

The whole world is a Christmas tree,
  And stars its many candles be.
Oh! sing a carol joyfully
  The year's great feast in keeping!

For once, on a December night
  An angel held a candle bright
And led three Wise Men by its light
  To where a Child was sleeping.

For Christmas

RACHEL FIELD

Now not a window small or big
But wears a wreath or holly sprig;
Nor any shop too poor to show
Its spray of pine or mistletoe.

Now city airs are spicy-sweet
With Christmas trees along each street,
Green spruce and fir whose boughs will hold
Their tinseled balls and fruits of gold.

Now postmen pass in threes and fours
Like bent, blue-coated Santa Claus.
Now people hurry to and fro
With little girls and boys in tow,

And not a child but keeps some trace
Of Christmas secrets in his face.

A Catch by the Hearth

AUTHOR UNKNOWN

Sing we all merrily
Christmas is here,
The day that we love best
Of days in the year.

Bring forth the holly,
The box, and the bay,
Deck out our cottage
For glad Christmas Day.

Sing we all merrily,
Draw around the fire,
Sister and brother,
Grandsire, and sire.

The Holly and the Ivy

Traditional English

Traditional English,
collected and arranged by Cecil J. Sharp

The hol-ly and the i - vy, when they are both full

grown, of all the trees that are in the wood, the hol-ly bears the

crown. The rising of the sun and the running of the

deer, the playing of the merry organ, sweet singing in the choir.

The holly bears a blossom as white as lily flow'r,
And Mary bore sweet Jesus Christ to be our sweet Savior.

The rising of the sun and the running of the deer,
The playing of the merry organ, sweet singing in the choir.

The holly bears a berry as red as any blood,
And Mary bore sweet Jesus Christ to do poor sinners good.

The rising of the sun and the running of the deer,
The playing of the merry organ, sweet singing in the choir.

The Old Christmas Bell

J. FRANCIS THOMAS

There is a little Christmas bell
Which hangs upon our tree;
It first was hung for Great-Grandma
When she was only three.

Each year it's hung upon the tree
With care and much delight;
For generations it has seen
So many Christmas nights.

What stories this small bell could tell
Of trees with candlelight,
Of homemade trimmings, and the gifts
Wrapped in those colors bright.

For all those generations past,
This little bell survived;
And many who enjoyed it so
No longer are alive.

But every year with care it's wrapped
And carefully put away
To be brought forth for memories
On another Christmas Day.

To a Christmas Tree

FRANCES FROST

O balsam tree, that lately held
The stars like nesting birds among
Your emerald branches, listen now
To children's voices sweet with song!

You, talker with the wind and friend
Of fox and fawn and silver mouse,
Bearing your tinsel and your gifts,
Glow softly now within this house,

Bringing your fragrance to our hearts,
Assuring us that wars will cease.
For a Child's bright birthday, shine with faith,
O tree, and loveliness and peace!

Christmas Tree

LAURENCE SMITH

Star over all,
Eye of the night,
Stand on my tree,
Magical sight,
Green under frost,
Green under snow,
Green under tinsel,
Glitter and glow,
Appled with baubles,
Silver and gold,
Spangled with fire,
Warm over cold.

THE BEST TREE EVER

Clancy Strock

As you'll recall while reading the next several pages, every family has its own special way of enjoying the Christmas tree.

First is the matter of when your tree goes up. In some families, this happens soon after Thanksgiving, so the tree can be enjoyed for a whole month. In other homes, decorating the tree is a Christmas Eve tradition. Everyone pitches in while sampling Mom's array of Christmas cookies washed down with eggnog.

Then there are families with little children who wake up on Christmas morning to the miracle of not only presents, but a fully decorated tree that wondrously appeared overnight.

We were a "Christmas Eve" family while I was growing up, but I think it was more out of economic necessity than anything else. Dad would wait until suppertime on the night before Christmas, then drive over to see the tree vendors when they were ready to close up and go home. If they'd been lucky, only a few scraggly, deformed, lopsided trees remained on the lot.

Dad would pick out the best of the rejects, offer the man twenty-five cents, tie it to the roof of our Willys, and head home. Once there, he'd spend an hour creating a tree we could be proud of. He'd prune here and lop off a branch there, then use a drill to insert them in spaces that needed help. Only God can make a tree, but Oscar Strock didn't shy away from offering a helping hand.

He'd haul the tree into the living room, then slowly rotate it until Mom decided how it looked best. Even with all his work, there was always an ugly side that needed to be hidden.

Dad was also in charge of putting up the lights. If one bulb on the string was loose or blown, the whole works went out. When that happened, Dad set to the tedious task of hunting down the bad bulb, starting at one end and, bulb by bulb, testing each socket with a new bulb.

No matter which end he started with, the dead bulb was always at the other end. To make matters worse, he had wired several strings together. Instead of checking a dozen bulbs, he had to work his way through fifty or sixty.

Both Mom and Dad remembered their own childhood trees, which, by the way, were illuminated with real candles.

When the lights were in place and working, Mom, my sister, and I would hang the ornaments. Mostly they were more fragile than eggshells and shattered into scores of tiny pieces when dropped. The sturdier ones went on the lower branches, and any cat owner knows why. Cats love to practice their

tennis serves on Christmas ornaments.

In those Depression days, people made many of their own decorations. We strung popcorn and cranberries on strong thread. It was slow work, but it kept us kids busy for hours. We also made paper chains with red, green, and white paper, gluing each link together with flour-and-water paste.

One year we tried marshmallows for ornaments. As they gradually vanished, Mom blamed Mary and me. We denied everything, pointing out Dad's fondness for marshmallows. He blamed the cat.

Ornaments could also be made from walnut shell halves painted gold or silver, or pinecones with paint-frosted edges. People living near south-Atlantic beaches collected sand dollars which, with a little paint, became elegant decorations.

One Christmas tree ornament I miss is the old-time tinfoil icicle. Today's plastic stuff doesn't have enough weight to hang right and slips off the tree every time someone walks by. Besides, you can't pick it off the tree and save it for next year.

The final touch was the small spiky ornament that slipped over the topmost twig to crown the tree.

Finally, we'd plop down in chairs and silently admire the tree. Soon someone would sigh and say, "That's the best tree ever!" And we'd all agree—until next year.

Christmas Cheer

ALICE WILLIAMS BROTHERTON

The Holly, oh, the Holly!
Green leaf, and berry red,
Is the plant that thrives in winter,
When all the rest are fled.

When snows are on the ground,
And the skies are gray and drear,
The Holly comes at Christmastide
And brings the Christmas cheer.

Sing the Mistletoe, the Ivy,
And the Holly bush so gay
That come to us in winter—
No summer friends are they.

Give me the sturdy friendship
That will ever loyal hold,
And give me the hardy Holly
That dares the winter's cold;

Oh, the roses bloom in June,
When the skies are bright and clear;
But the Holly comes at Christmastide,
The best time o' the year.

Sing the Holly, and the Ivy,
And the merry Mistletoe
That come to us in winter,
When the fields are white with snow!

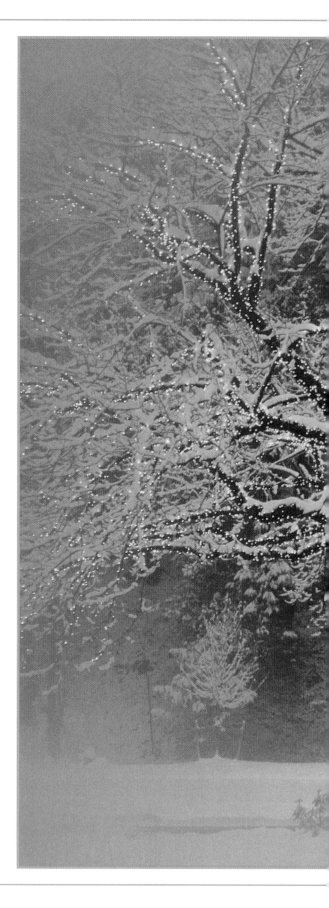

'Neath Mistletoe

J. ASHBY STERRY

'Neath mistletoe, should chance arise,
You may be happy if you're wise,
Though bored you lie with pantomime
And Christmas fare and Christmas rhyme.

One fine old custom don't despise;
If you're a man of enterprise,
You'll find, I venture to surmise,
'Tis pleasant then at Christmastime
    'Neath mistletoe!

You see they scarcely can disguise
The sparkle of their pretty eyes;
And no one thinks it is a crime,
When goes the merry Christmas chime,
A rare old rite to exercise
    'Neath mistletoe!

Mistletoe

WALTER DE LA MARE

Sitting under the mistletoe
(Pale-green, fairy mistletoe),
One last candle burning low,
All the sleepy dancers gone,
Just one candle burning on,
Shadows lurking everywhere:
Someone came and kissed me there.

Tired I was; my head would go
Nodding under the mistletoe
(Pale-green, fairy mistletoe);
No footsteps came, no voice, but only,
Just as I sat there, sleepy, lonely,
Stooped in the still and shadowy air
Lips unseen—and kissed me there.

Deck the Halls with Greenery and Lights

*B*ut give me holly, bold and jolly,
Honest, prickly, shining holly;
Pluck me holly leaf and berry
For the day when I make merry.

—Christina G. Rossetti

Best of all are the decorations the grandchildren have made—fat little stars and rather crooked Santas, shaped out of dough and baked in the oven.

—Gladys Taber

*W*ith holly and ivy
So green and so gay
We deck up our houses
As fresh as the day;

With bay and rosemary
And laurel complete;
And everyone now
Is a queen in conceit.

—Author Unknown

*T*hen heigh ho! the holly!
This life is most jolly!

—William Shakespeare

The decoration of the Christmas tree has a pleasing, ritualistic quality about it, as favorite and forgotten decorations are once again greeted with joy. But a few always seem to have suffered from lying in a box throughout the year and new, exciting items are needed. Why not gilded walnuts?

—Author Unknown

So now is come our joyful feast,
Let every man be jolly;
Each room with ivy leaves is dressed
And every post with holly.

And while thus inspired we sing,
Let all the streets with echoes ring;
Woods and hills and everything
Bear witness we are merry.
—GEORGE WITHER

Choose wisely, then, each ornament and
frosted tinsel skein
For branches that have worn jewels
of gleaming mountain rain.
—ELIZABETH-ELLAN LONG

ALL YOUNG FIR TREES, as you know by that story of Hans Andersen's,
dream of being a Christmas tree someday. They dream about it as young
girls dream of being a bride, or young poets of having a volume of verse
published.

—CHRISTOPHER MORLEY

Candle, candle burning bright
On our windowsill tonight,
Like the shining Christmas star
Guiding shepherds from afar,
Lead some weary traveler here,
That he may share our Christmas cheer.
—ISABEL SHAW

Be merry all, be merry all,
With holly dress the festive hall;
Prepare the song, the feast, the ball,
To welcome merry Christmas all.
—W. R. SPENSER

PERHAPS THE BEST Yuletide decoration is being wreathed in smiles.
—AUTHOR UNKNOWN

MY FIRST CHRISTMAS TREE

Hamlin Garland

I will begin by saying that we never had a Christmas tree in our house in the Wisconsin coulee; indeed, my father never saw one in a family circle until he saw that which I set up for my own children last year. But we celebrated Christmas in those days, always, and I cannot remember a time when we did not all hang up our stockings for "Sandy Claws" to fill. As I look back upon those days, it seems as if the snows were always deep, the night skies crystal clear, and the stars especially lustrous with frosty sparkles of blue and yellow fire—and probably this was so, for we lived in a northern land where winter was usually stern and always long.

When I was ten years old, we moved to Mitchell County, an Iowa prairie land, and there we prospered in such wise that our stockings always held toys of some sort; and even my mother's stocking occasionally sagged with a simple piece of jewelry or a new comb or brush. But the thought of a family tree remained the luxury of millionaire city dwellers; indeed, it was not until my fifteenth or sixteenth year that our Sunday school rose to the extravagance of a tree, and it is of this wondrous festival that I write.

The land about us was only partly cultivated at this time, and our district schoolhouse, a bare little box, was set bleakly on the prairie. The Burr Oak schoolhouse was not only larger, but it stood beneath great oaks as well and possessed the charm of a forest background through which a stream ran silently. It was our chief social center. There, of a Sunday, a regular preacher held "Divine service" with Sunday school as a sequence. At night—usually on Friday nights—the young people let in "ly-ceums," as we called them, to debate great questions or to "speak pieces" and read essays; and here it was that I saw my first Christmas tree.

I walked to that tree across four miles of moonlit snow. Snow? No, it was a floor of diamonds, a magical world, so beautiful that my heart still aches with the wonder of it and with the regret that it has all gone— gone with the keen eyes and the bounding pulses of the boy.

Our home at this time was a small frame house on the prairie almost directly west of the Burr Oak grove; and as it was too cold to take the horses, my brother and I, with our tall boots, our visored caps, and our long woolen mufflers, started forth afoot defiant of the cold. We left the gate on the trot, bound for a sight of the glittering unknown. The snow was deep and we moved side by side in the grooves made by the hooves of horses, setting our feet in the shine left by the broad shoes of the wood sleighs whose going had smoothed the way for us.

Our breaths rose like smoke in the still air. It must have been ten below zero, but that did not trouble us in those days; and at last we came in sight of the lights, in sound of the singing, the laughter, the bells of the feast.

It was a poor little building without tower or bell, and its low walls had but three windows on a side. And yet it seemed very imposing to me that night as I crossed the threshold and faced the strange people who packed it to the door. I say "strange people," for though I had seen most of them many times, they all seemed somehow alien to me that night. I was an irregular attendant at Sunday school and did not expect a present; therefore, I stood against the wall and gazed with open-eyed marveling at the shining pine which stood where the pulpit was wont to be.

I don't think that the tree had many candles, and I don't remember that it glittered with golden apples. But it was loaded with presents.

A furious jingling of bells, a loud voice outside, the lifting of a window, the nearer clash of bells, and the dear old Saint appeared, clothed in a red robe, a belt of sleigh bells, and a long white beard. The children cried out, "Oh!" The girls tittered and shrieked with excitement, and the boys laughed and clapped their hands. Then "Sandy" made a little speech about being glad to see us all, but as he had many other

places to visit, as there were a great many presents to distribute, he guessed he'd have to ask some of the many pretty girls to help him. So he called upon Betty Burtch and Hattie Knapp—and I for one admired his taste, for they were the most popular maids of the school.

They came up blushing, and a little bewildered by the blaze of publicity thus blown upon them. But their native dignity asserted itself, and the distribution of the presents began. I have a notion now that the fruit upon the tree was mostly bags of popcorn and "corny copias" of candy; but as my brother and I stood there that night and saw everybody, even the rowdiest boy, getting something, we felt aggrieved and rebellious. We forgot that we had come from afar—we only knew that we were being left out.

But suddenly, in the midst of our gloom, my brother's name was called, and a lovely girl with a gentle smile handed him a bag of popcorn. My heart glowed with gratitude. Somebody had thought of us; and when she came to me, saying sweetly, "Here's something for you," I had not words to thank her. This happened nearly forty years ago, but her smile, her outstretched hand, her sympathetic eyes are vividly before me as I write. She was sorry for the shock-headed boy who stood against the wall, and her pity made the little box of candy a casket of pearls. The fact that I swallowed the jewels on the road home does not take from the reality of my adoration.

At last I had to take my final glimpse of that wondrous tree, and I well remember the walk home. My brother and I traveled in wordless companionship. The moon was sinking toward the west, and the snow crust gleamed with a million fairy lamps. The sentinel watchdogs barked from lonely farmhouses, and the wolves answered from the ridges. Now and then sleighs passed us with lovers sitting two and two, and the bells on their horses had the remote music of romance to us whose boots drummed like clogs of wood upon the icy road.

Our house was dark as we approached and entered it, but how deliciously warm it seemed after the pitiless wind! I confess we made straight for the cupboard for a mince pie, a doughnut, and a bowl of milk.

As I write this, there stands in my library a thick-branched, beautifully tapering fir tree covered with the gold and purple apples of Hesperides, together with crystal ice points, green and red and yellow candles, clusters of gilded grapes, wreaths of metallic frost, and glittering angels swinging in ecstasy; but I doubt if my children will ever know the keen pleasure (that is almost pain) which came to my brother and to me in those Christmas days when an orange was not a breakfast fruit, but a casket of incense and of spice, a message of the sunlands of the South.

Sweets That Deck the Table

Holly-Trimmed Cookie Bars

Preheat oven to 350°F. In a medium mixing bowl, sift together 1 cup all-purpose flour, 1 teaspoon baking powder, and ½ teaspoon salt. Set aside. In a large bowl, cream ½ cup butter, ½ cup granulated sugar, and 1 cup brown sugar until light. Stir in 1 egg and ½ cup evaporated milk. Add 1 cup oats. Add flour mixture; beat until well blended. Add 1 cup chopped pecans or walnuts, 1 cup chopped dates, and ¼ cup chopped candied fruit; stir until evenly distributed. Spread mixture in a greased 13- x 9- x 2-inch baking pan. Bake 45 to 50 minutes. Cool thoroughly.

In a small bowl, whisk together 1 cup sifted powdered sugar, ¼ teaspoon salt, 2 tablespoons milk, and ½ teaspoon vanilla extract. Drizzle glaze over bars; cut into 2-inch squares. Decorate with red and green candied cherries. Makes 24 cookie bars.

CINNAMON CHRISTMAS TREE

Preheat oven to 350°F. In a small bowl, combine 2 tablespoons granulated sugar and ½ teaspoon cinnamon. On wax paper, unroll dough from one 8-ounce can refrigerated crescent rolls into one large rectangle and seal perforations by pinching dough. Spread 2 tablespoons softened butter evenly over dough. Sprinkle cinnamon-sugar mixture and 2 tablespoons raisins evenly over dough. Roll rectangle up tightly, starting from a long side. Slice roll into 16 equal pieces. On a greased cookie sheet, arrange slices in a triangular pattern, starting with 1 slice at the top, 2 slices in the second row, 3 slices in the third row, and so on, reserving 1 slice to form the tree stem at the bottom. Bake 20 to 25 minutes.

In a small bowl, combine ¾ cup powdered sugar and enough milk, about 2 tablespoons, to make a glaze. Drizzle glaze over warm rolls. Decorate with red and green candies or candied fruit; serve warm. Makes 16 rolls.

CANDY CHRISTMAS WREATH

In a large saucepan over low heat, melt ½ cup butter. Add one 10-ounce package of marshmallows; stir constantly until marshmallows are melted and smooth. Remove from heat and add green food coloring to desired shade of green. Gently stir in 6 cups of cornflakes, mixing thoroughly. With buttered fingers, lightly press entire mixture into a buttered 8-cup ring mold. Cool 2 minutes and turn out onto a serving plate. Decorate with red cinnamon candies. Makes one 10-inch wreath.

In the living room, golden lights twinkle in the branches of the Christmas tree. Fresh holly nestles among the candles on the mantel, as garland sweeps around the banisters and over the entryways. From the kitchen comes the sweet aroma of freshly made cookies and candy, laid out in rows to cool.

The Christmas Holly

ELIZA COOK

The holly! The holly! Oh, twine it with bay—
Come give the holly a song;
For it helps to drive stern winter away,
With his garment so somber and long;

It peeps through the trees with its berries of red
And its leaves of burnished green,
When the flowers and fruits have long been dead,
And not even the daisy is seen.

Then sing to the holly, the Christmas holly,
That hangs over peasant and king;
While we laugh and carouse 'neath its
     glittering boughs,
To the Christmas holly we'll sing.

The gale may whistle, the frost may come
To fetter the gurgling rill;
The woods may be bare and warblers dumb,
But holly is beautiful still.

In the revel and light of princely halls
The bright holly branch is found;
And its shadow falls on the lowliest walls,
While the brimming horn goes round.

The ivy lives long, but its home must be
Where graves and ruins are spread;
There's beauty about the cypress tree,
But it flourishes near the dead;

The laurel the warrior's brow may wreathe,
But it tells of tears and blood;
I sing to the holly, and who can breathe
Aught of that that is not good?

Then sing to the holly, the Christmas holly,
That hangs over peasant and king;
While we laugh and carouse 'neath
     its glittering boughs,
To the Christmas holly we'll sing.

Winter Evergreens

J. E. CARPENTER

The roses long have passed their prime,
The fruits no more are seen,
So let us chime a Christmas rhyme to hail
     the Evergreen—the Evergreen!

Though bright may be the summer wreath,
To mourn it were but folly,
While friends delight to meet beneath
     the Mistletoe—the Mistletoe and Holly!

Then circle round the ruddy blaze
And let but mirth be seen,
We still can raise a song of praise
     to hail—to hail the Evergreen!

What though we rove the woods no more,
Some love to sing the joys of spring, with them
     why need we quarrel
While jovial Christmas deigns to bring the Ivy—
     the Ivy and the Laurel?

Then let us all each other aid where friendship's
     wreath is seen,
'Tis never made of flowers that fade, but of
     the Evergreen;
'Tis never made of flowers that fade, but of
     the Evergreen!

CHAPTER TWO

The Joy of Gifts

If you see a package
Gaily wrapped and tied,
Don't ask too many questions,
'Cause a secret is inside.

—E. KATHRYN FOWLER

Christmas Gifts

EDNA JAQUES

I'd like a little china shoe,
With painted heels and bows of blue
And pink and blue forget-me-nots
And little clumps of golden dots,

Some lavender to shed perfume
In every corner of my room,
A pair of shoe trees painted pink,
New curtains for above the sink,

Some Christmas greens to decorate
The tall white pillars by the gate,

Fresh cedars, stalks of spicy pine,
A scarlet Merry Christmas sign,

A box of jam in fancy jars,
Some peppermints and chocolate bars,
Some candied ginger and a few
Old-fashioned gingersnaps to chew,

And oh, a star above the town
With Christmas carols drifting down,
A snow-clad street—for such as these
I will be more than thankful, please.

Christmas List

HILDA BUTLER FARR

What do we want for Christmas?
What do we want, indeed.
We're well supplied with comforts;
There's little that we need.

What are we most desiring
As carols flood the air?
What do we want for Christmas
To lift our souls from care?

A little understanding,
Some love and friendship too,
Some kindly words to help us
In everything we do.

These lasting gifts of beauty
We'd choose above the rest;
They're all we need for Christmas
To make us rich and blessed.

The Twelve Days of Christmas

TRADITIONAL

TRADITIONAL

On the first day of Christmas, my true love sent to me a

par - tridge in a pear tree. On the second day of Christmas, my

true love sent to me two turtle doves and a partridge in a pear

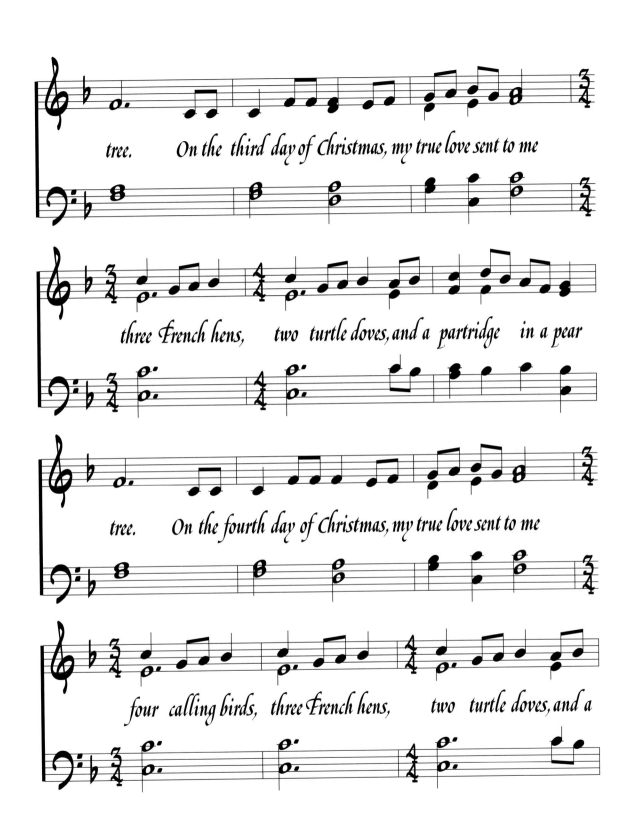

partridge in a pear tree. On the fifth day of Christmas, my

true love sent to me five gol-den rings,

four calling birds, three French hens, two turtle doves,

and a par-tridge in a pear tree. On the

sixth day of Christmas, my true love sent to me
seventh day of Christmas, my true love sent to me
eighth day of Christmas, my true love sent to me
ninth day of Christmas, my true love sent to me
tenth day of Christmas, my true love sent to me
eleventh day of Christmas, my true love sent to me
twelfth day of Christmas, my true love sent to me

six geese a-laying, five gol-den rings,
seven swans a-swimming,
eight maids a-milking,
nine ladies dancing,
ten lords a-leaping,
eleven pipers piping,
twelve drummers drumming,

four calling birds, three French hens, two turtle doves, and a

par-tridge in a pear tree. On the tree.

6.-11. 12.

Christmas Shopping

ISLA PASCHAL RICHARDSON

I came upon her suddenly as she, in
    placid reverie,
Sat gazing on the hurrying crowd outside
    the windows of a shop
Bedecked in glistening holly wreaths.
Long golden curls and eyes of china blue.
My eyes met hers and smiled.
So many years have dolls and I conspired
    on Christmas Eve,
And this one, just the size for little arms.
(I see a dimpled hand upraised lest I
Awake the doll that's being rocked to sleep.)

The crowd is jostling me, and I, remembering,
Retrace my steps.
It was the shop next door I wanted—
Sporting Goods—that's it.
(And now I see a tall slim form,
The lithe, athletic lankness of a growing girl
Whose sparkling eyes laugh in life's face.)
Oh, yes, a tennis racket—that was on my list.
But entering, I cast a backward, wistful glance
Where gaze blue china eyes
Serene and smiling on a hurrying world.

Christmas Giving

IRIS W. BRAY

Christmas is for giving
And showing that we care,
For honoring the Christ Child
With the loving gifts we share.

The Wise Men gave of riches;
The shepherds, faith and love.
Each gift, in its own measure,
Was smiled on from above.

Let every gift be treasured;
Not always size or price

Determines the extent of love
And willing sacrifice.

Handsome gifts with festive trim
Bring smiles of sweet content,
But modest gifts of humble means
Are ofttimes heaven sent.

Whether it be large or small,
Each gift will share in part
The message of true Christmas joy
If given from the heart!

THE GIFT OF THE MAGI

O. Henry

One dollar and eighty-seven cents. That was all. And sixty cents of it was in pennies. Pennies saved one and two at a time by bulldozing the grocer and the vegetable man and the butcher until one's cheeks burned with the silent imputation of parsimony that such close dealing implied. Three times Della counted it. One dollar and eighty-seven cents. And the next day would be Christmas.

There was clearly nothing to do but flop down on the shabby little couch and howl. So Della did it. Which instigates the moral reflection that life is made up of sobs, sniffles, and smiles, with sniffles predominating.

While the mistress of the home is gradually subsiding from the first stage to the second, take a look at the home. A furnished flat at eight dollars per week. It did not exactly beggar description, but it certainly had that word on the lookout for the mendicancy squad.

In the vestibule below was a letterbox into which no letter would go, and an electric button from which no mortal finger could coax a ring. Also pertaining thereunto was a card bearing the name, "Mr. James Dillingham Young."

The "Dillingham" had been flung to the breeze during a former period of prosperity when its possessor was being paid thirty dollars per week. Now, when the income was shrunk to twenty dollars, the letters of "Dillingham" looked blurred, as though they were thinking seriously of contracting to a modest and unassuming D. But whenever Mr. James Dillingham Young came home and reached his flat above he was called "Jim" and greatly hugged by Mrs. James Dillingham Young, already introduced to you as Della. Which is all very good.

Della finished her cry and attended to her cheeks with the powder rag. She stood by the window and looked out dully at a gray cat walking a gray fence in a gray backyard. Tomorrow would be Christmas Day, and she had only a dollar and eighty-seven cents with which to buy Jim a present. She had been saving every penny she could for months, with this result. Twenty dollars a week doesn't go far. Expenses had been greater than she had calculated. They always are. Only a dollar and eighty-seven cents to buy a present for Jim. Her Jim. Many a happy hour she had spent planning for something nice for him. Something fine and rare and sterling—something just a little bit near to being worthy of the honor of being owned by Jim.

There was a pier glass between the windows of the room. Perhaps you have seen a pier-glass in an eight dollar flat. A very thin and very agile person may, by observing his reflection in a rapid sequence of longitudinal strips, obtain a fairly accurate conception of his looks. Della, being slender, had mastered the art.

Suddenly she whirled from the window and stood before the glass. Her eyes were shining brilliantly, but her face had lost its color within twenty seconds. Rapidly she pulled down her hair and let it fall to its full length.

Now, there were two possessions of the James Dillingham Youngs in which they both took a mighty pride. One was Jim's gold watch that had been his father's and his grandfather's. The other was Della's hair.

Had the Queen of Sheba lived in the flat across the airshaft, Della would have let her hair hang out the window someday to dry just to deprecate Her Majesty's jewels and gifts. Had King Solomon been the janitor, with all his treasures piled up in the basement, Jim would have pulled out his watch every time he passed, just to see him pluck at his beard from envy.

So now Della's beautiful hair fell about her, rippling and shining like a cascade of brown waters. It reached below her knee and made itself almost a garment for her. And then she did it up again nervously and quickly. Once she faltered for a minute and stood still while a tear or two splashed on the worn red carpet.

On went her old brown jacket; on went her old brown hat. With a whirl of skirts and with the brilliant sparkle still in her eyes, she fluttered out the door and down the stairs to the street.

Where she stopped the sign read: "Mme. Sofronie. Hair Goods of All Kinds." One flight up Della ran, and collected herself, panting. Madame, large, too white, chilly, hardly looked the "Sofronie."

"Will you buy my hair?" asked Della.

"I buy hair," said Madame. "Take yer hat off and let's have a sight at the looks of it."

Down rippled the brown cascade.

"Twenty dollars," said Madame, lifting the mass with a practiced hand.

"Give it to me quick," said Della.

Oh, and the next two hours tripped by on rosy wings. Forget the hashed metaphor. She was ransacking the stores for Jim's present.

She found it at last. It surely had been made for Jim and no one else. There was no other like it in any of the stores, and she had turned all of them inside out. It was a platinum fob chain simple and chaste in design, properly proclaiming its value by substance alone and not by meretricious ornamentation—as all good things should do. It was even worthy of The Watch. As soon as she saw it she knew that it must be Jim's. It was like him. Quietness and value—the description applied to both. Twenty-one dollars they took from her for it, and she hurried home with the eighty-seven cents. With that chain on his watch Jim might be properly anxious about the time in any company. Grand as the watch was, he sometimes looked at it on the sly on account of the old leather strap that he used in place of a chain.

When Della reached home her intoxication gave way a little to prudence and reason. She got out her curling irons and lighted the gas and went to work repairing the ravages made by generosity added to love. Which is always a treacherous task, dear friends—a mammoth task.

Within forty minutes her head was covered with tiny, close-lying curls that made her look wonderfully like a truant schoolboy. She looked at her reflection in the mirror long, carefully, and critically.

"If Jim doesn't kill me," she said to herself,

"before he takes a second look at me, he'll say I look like a Coney Island chorus girl. But what could I do—oh! what could I do with a dollar and eighty-seven cents?"

At seven o'clock the coffee was made and the frying pan was on the back of the stove hot and ready to cook the chops.

Jim was never late. Della doubled the fob chain in her hand and sat on the corner of the table near the door that he always entered. Then she heard his step on the stair away down on the first flight, and she turned white for just a moment. She had a habit for saying little silent prayers about the simplest everyday things, and now she whispered: "Please God, make him think I am still pretty."

The door opened and Jim stepped in and closed it. He looked thin and very serious. Poor fellow, he was only twenty-two—and to be burdened with a family! He needed a new overcoat and he was without gloves.

Jim stopped inside the door, as immovable as a setter at the scent of quail. His eyes were fixed upon Della, and there was an expression in them that she could not read, and it terrified her. It was not anger, nor surprise, nor disapproval, nor horror, nor any of the sentiments that she had been prepared for. He simply stared at her fixedly with that peculiar expression on his face.

Della wriggled off the table and went for him.

"Jim, darling," she cried, "don't look at me that way. I had my hair cut off and sold because I couldn't have lived through Christmas without giving you a present. It'll grow out again—you won't mind, will you? I just had to do it. My hair grows awfully fast. Say 'Merry Christmas!' Jim, and let's be happy. You don't know what a nice—what a beautiful, nice gift I've got for you."

"You've cut off your hair?" asked Jim, laboriously, as if he had not arrived at that patent fact yet even after the hardest mental labor.

"Cut it off and sold it," said Della. "Don't you like me just as well, anyhow? I'm me without my hair, ain't I?"

Jim looked about the room curiously.

"You say your hair is gone?" he said, with an air almost of idiocy.

"You needn't look for it," said Della. "It's sold, I tell you—sold and gone, too. It's Christmas Eve, boy. Be good to me, for it went for you. Maybe the hairs of my head were numbered," she went on with sudden serious sweetness, "but nobody could ever count my love for you. Shall I put the chops on, Jim?"

Out of his trance Jim seemed quickly to wake. He enfolded his Della. For ten seconds let us regard with discreet scrutiny some inconsequential object in the other direction. Eight dollars a week or a million a year—what is the difference? A mathematician or a wit would give you the wrong answer. The Magi brought valuable gifts, but that was not among them. This dark assertion will be illuminated later on.

Jim drew a package from his overcoat

pocket and threw it upon the table. Don't make any mistake, Dell," he said, "about me. I don't think there's anything in the way of a haircut or a shave or a shampoo that could make me like my girl any less. But if you'll unwrap that package you may see why you had me going a while at first."

White fingers and nimble tore at the string and paper. And then an ecstatic scream of joy; and then, alas! a quick feminine change to hysterical tears and wails, necessitating the immediate employment of all the comforting powers of the lord of the flat.

For there lay The Combs—the set of combs, side and back, that Della had worshiped long in a Broadway window. Beautiful combs, pure tortoise shell, with jeweled rims—just the shade to wear in the beautiful vanished hair. They were expensive combs, she knew, and her heart had simply craved and yearned over them without the least hope of possession. And now, they were hers, but the tresses that should have adorned the coveted adornments were gone.

But she hugged them to her bosom, and at length she was able to look up with dim eyes and a smile and say: "My hair grows so fast, Jim!"

And then Della leaped up like a little singed cat and cried, "Oh, oh!"

Jim had not yet seen his beautiful present. She held it out to him eagerly upon her open palm. The dull precious metal seemed to flash with a reflection of her bright and ardent spirit.

"Isn't it a dandy, Jim? I hunted all over town to find it. You'll have to look at the time a hundred times a day now. Give me your watch. I want to see how it looks on it."

Instead of obeying, Jim tumbled down on the couch and put his hands under the back of his head and smiled.

"Dell," said he, "let's put our Christmas presents away and keep 'em a while. They're too nice to use just at present. I sold the watch to get the money to buy your combs. And now suppose you put the chops on."

The Magi, as you know, were wise men—wonderfully wise men—who brought gifts to the Babe in the manger. They invented the art of giving Christmas presents. Being wise, their gifts were no doubt wise ones, possibly bearing the privilege of exchange in case of duplication. And here I have lamely related to you the uneventful chronicle of two foolish children in a flat who most unwisely sacrificed for each other the greatest treasures of their house. But in a last word to the wise of these days let it be said that of all who give gifts these two were the wisest. Of all who give and receive gifts, such as they are wisest. Everywhere they are wisest. They are the magi.

Through a Shop Window

ELEANOR FARJEON

How full the glittering shops are now
With chattering tongues and open purses,
And children scrambling anyhow
Beside their mothers, aunts, and nurses;
With eager eyes and laughing lips,
And problems of a thousand choices,
With loaded trees, and lucky dips,
And Christmastime in all the voices!
You scarce can push your way along
Behind the window—which discloses
Outside the little ragged throng
With longing eyes and flattened noses.

Christmas Shoppers

AILEEN FISHER

Oh, the wind is brisk and biting
and the cold is not inviting,
but there's music, merry music everywhere.

The streets are full of bustle,
and our feet are full of hustle,
for there's Christmas, merry Christmas
    in the air.

Oh, the wind is cold and chilly
and it whistles at us shrilly,
but there's music, merry music everywhere.

The bells are full of ringing
and our hearts are full of singing,
for there's Christmas, merry Christmas
    in the air.

Eighth Street West

RACHEL FIELD

I will go walking on Eighth Street
    Now that it's Christmastime
To see the little shops all decked
    Gay as a pantomime.

There will be patchwork and Russian smocks;
    Angels of marzipan;
Green glass bottles and picture books
    In their jackets, spick-and-span.

There will be knickknacks of painted wood;
    Candles for every tree
Stacked at the curb in spicy green
    Bristling and needly.

There will be children and dogs about;
    Organ men to play;
And people carrying parcels home,
    Hurrying on their way.

I will go walking on Eighth Street
    From Avenue to L,
Seeing the sights of Christmas,
    Smelling each Christmas smell.

Special Surprises for Family and Friends

It always sets me wondering;
For whether it is thin or wide
You never know just what's inside.

Especially on Christmas week,
Temptation is so great to peek!
Now wouldn't it be much more fun
If shoppers carried things undone?

—JOHN FARRAR

LOVE IS NOT getting, but giving.

—HENRY VAN DYKE

CHRISTMAS IS NOT a time nor a season, but a state of mind.
To cherish peace and goodwill, to be plenteous in mercy, is to
have the real spirit of Christmas.

—CALVIN COOLIDGE

HE WHO HAS not Christmas in his heart will never find it under a tree.

—ROY L. SMITH

YOU GIVE but little when you give of your
possessions. It is when you give of yourself
that you truly give.

—KAHLIL GIBRAN

Shake-shake,
Shake the package well.

But what there is
Inside of it,
Shaking will not tell.

—JAMES S. TIPPETT

ONE DAY, a six-year-old boy in a Southern town answered a knock at the door. It was his father, just returned from Southeast Asia. He didn't ask, "Daddy, what did you bring me?" He threw his arms around his father's neck and said, "Oh, Daddy, this is the best Christmas present I've ever had!"

—BILLY GRAHAM

IT IS MORE blessed to give than to receive.

—ACTS 20:35

What can I give Him,
Poor as I am?
If I were a shepherd
I would bring a lamb;
If I were a Wise Man
I would do my part—
Yet what I can, I give Him,
Give my heart.

—CHRISTINA G. ROSSETTI

Of all the gifts that Christmas brings,
The best are made of little things:

Melody of carols all year,
Cheer to friends that you hold dear.

—ALBERTA DREDLA

THE BEST of all gifts around any Christmas tree: the presence of a happy family all wrapped up in each other.

—BURTON HILLIS

CHRISTMAS IS MORE than a gift-laden tree; it is caring and sharing unselfishly.

—LAURA BAKER HAYNES

CHRISTMAS GIFTS FROM THE KITCHEN

JELLY JEWELS

In a medium bowl, cream ½ cup softened butter with ¼ cup brown sugar. Stir in 1 cup all-purpose flour. Add 1 teaspoon vanilla extract. Separate 1 egg; set white aside. Beat egg yolk; add to flour mixture and mix well. Chill at least 30 minutes.

Preheat oven to 325°F. Beat egg white in small bowl. Measure ¾ cup ground walnuts into separate small bowl. Form dough into small balls; roll each in egg white and then in nuts. Place on cookie sheet and bake 5 minutes. Remove from oven and press an indentation in center of each cookie. Return to oven and bake 10 to 15 minutes longer or until edges are lightly browned. Remove to wire rack to cool; fill each indentation with ¼ teaspoon jelly. Makes 2 dozen cookies.

CRANBERRY-APPLE MINI LOAVES

Preheat oven to 350°F. In a medium mixing bowl, sift together 1½ cups all-purpose flour, 1 cup granulated sugar, 1 teaspoon ground cinnamon, ½ teaspoon baking soda, ¼ teaspoon salt, ¼ teaspoon baking powder, and ¼ teaspoon ground allspice. Set aside. In a small mixing bowl, combine ½ cup whole cranberry sauce, ½ cup chopped pecans, and ½ teaspoon finely grated orange peel; set aside. In a separate medium mixing bowl, whisk together 1 beaten egg, ½ cup finely shredded, peeled apple, and ¼ cup cooking oil. Make a well in the center of flour mixture and pour egg mixture into well. Stir just until moistened. Pour half of batter into 4 greased 4½- x 2½- x 1½-inch individual loaf pans (about ⅓ cup each pan). Spoon 2 tablespoons of cranberry mixture evenly over batter in each pan. Top with remaining batter and spoon remaining cranberry mixture down the center of each loaf. Bake until golden brown and a toothpick inserted in the center comes out clean, about 35 to 40 minutes. Remove to rack and cool 10 minutes; turn out onto serving platter. In a small mixing bowl, stir together ½ cup of sifted powdered sugar and enough orange juice, about 1 to 2 tablespoons, to make an icing of drizzling consistency. Drizzle over warm loaves. When cool, wrap in plastic wrap and tie up with ribbon to give as gifts. Makes 4 small loaves.

ROSEMARY AND LIME VINEGAR

In a non-corrosive saucepan, slowly bring to a boil 4¼ cups of a good white vinegar and 4 large sprigs fresh rosemary. Boil 1 minute; remove from heat. Let stand overnight.

Into decorative, sterilized bottles, place 4 fresh sprigs rosemary, 2 to 3 peeled and sliced garlic cloves, and 1 quartered or sliced lime. Strain vinegar; pour into bottles and seal. Store in a cool, dry place for at least 2 weeks to mature. Keeps for at least 6 months. Makes 4¼ cups.

Shopping bags bursting with boxes fill the corner of the room. A willow basket on the table holds rolls of shiny paper, spools of bright red ribbon, scissors, and tape. On the oak chair by the door sit clusters of jars, baskets, and fabric-wrapped bundles, waiting for delivery to friends and neighbors.

All the Days of Christmas

PHYLLIS McGINLEY

What shall my true love have from me
To pleasure his Christmas wealthily?
The partridge has flown from our pear tree.
Flown with our summers are the swans and
    the geese.
Milkmaids and drummers would leave him
    little peace.
I've no gold ring and no turtledove,

So what can I bring to my true love?
A coat for the drizzle chosen at the store;
A saw and a chisel for mending the door;
A pair of red slippers to slip on his feet;
Three striped neckties; something sweet.
He shall have all I can best afford—

No pipers piping, no leaping lord,
But a fine fat hen for his Christmas board;
Two pretty daughters (versed in the role)
To be worn like pinks in his buttonhole;
And the tree of my heart with its calling linnet—
My evergreen heart and the bright bird in it.

CHAPTER THREE

The Joy of Love

May you have the
    gladness of Christmas,
Which is hope;
The spirit of Christmas,
Which is peace;
The heart of Christmas,
Which is love.

—ADA V. HENDRICKS

27 Dec05

ALFRED DICKE LIBRARY
Box 2140
Jamestown ND 58402 2140

The Priceless Gift

A. G. AND RENA SEAVER

When Christmas came, long years ago,
On all mankind it did bestow
The Priceless Gift of love and cheer
With boundless hope for all the year.

This wondrous gift with which we live
The greater grows the more we give,
So let us share our joys with you
And bid despair and gloom adieu.

Somehow Not Only for Christmas

JOHN GREENLEAF WHITTIER

Somehow not only for Christmas
    But all the long year through,
The joy that you give to others
    Is the joy that comes back to you.

And the more you spend in blessing
    The poor and lonely and sad,
The more of your heart's possessing
    Returns to make you glad.

Where Love Might Enter In

KATE DOUGLAS WIGGIN

The door is on the latch tonight,
    The hearth-fire is aglow,
I seem to hear soft passing feet—
    The Christ Child in the snow.

My heart is open wide tonight
    For stranger, kith, or kin.
I would not bar a single door
    Where Love might enter in.

Here We Come A-Caroling

TRADITIONAL TRADITIONAL

Here we come a - car - o - ling a-

mong the leaves so green;

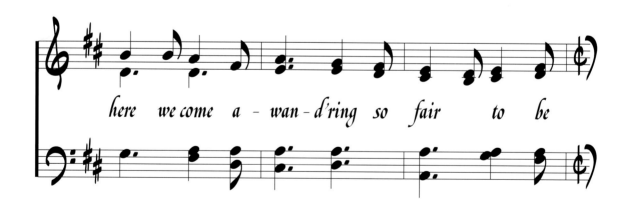

here we come a - wan - d'ring so fair to be

Holy Night

Walter Hard

As Doctor Stevens came into the village,
He let his horse slow down to a walk.
The moon broke through the clouds.
There was not a track on the new-fallen snow.
He was thinking how nice it was that the Judson
   baby had come on Christmas Eve.
He smiled his pleasant smile as he passed lighted
   houses with trimmed trees inside.
What could Ellen Hicks be doing up at this
   late hour?
She didn't have anyone to be filling stockings for.
Poor thing! She didn't have anything to fill a
   stocking with.
A shadow moved regularly across the drawn
   shade.

She was sitting there rocking—rocking.
The village clock struck eleven.
From the south came the faint tinkle of
   sleigh bells.
The snow creaked as he went up the steps.
The rocking stopped.
The light moved through the door into
   the hall.
Ellen unlocked the door. She held up the light
   to see who her late caller was.
She had a worn patchwork quilt around her
   shoulders.
The doctor went over to the chunk stove to
   warm his hands.
It gave out no heat. He touched it. It was
   barely warm.

No, of course there wasn't anything the matter
   with her.
She always sat up until midnight on Christmas Eve.
She'd got to thinking about that Stebbins family,
   and sat there rocking and forgot her fire.
How they could get along with all those young
   ones, and him all crippled, she couldn't see.
They didn't even have wood to keep them warm.
"Ellen, have you been giving wood to the
   Stebbinses?"
She admitted she had called the boy in and loaded
   his sled.
Well, maybe she had sent some food. Little by
   little the truth came out.
Her nephew did look after her; he always had.
But he'd told her she'd got to stop this sharing.
She'd promised.

But she couldn't bear to think of those Stebbinses.
She could get along. She still had wood in the shed.
The doctor's scolding stuck in his throat.
He went to the shed and brought in the last
   armful of wood.
He shut the stable door. He stopped to look down
   on the sleeping village.
So Ellen had to share. He recalled the look on
   her face.
Sharing. That was what Christmas meant.
The clock in the village struck twelve. Down in
   the valley a rooster crowed.
Overhead the moon moved slowly across the
   winter sky.
Holy night. Peaceful night.

PAPA PANOV'S
SPECIAL CHRISTMAS

Leo Tolstoy

It was Christmas Eve and although it was still afternoon, lights had begun to appear in the shops and houses of the little Russian village, for the short winter day was nearly over. Excited children scurried indoors and now only the muffled sounds of chatter and laughter escaped the closed shutters.

Old Papa Panov, the village shoemaker, stepped outside his shop to take one last look around. The sounds of happiness, the bright lights and the faint but delicious smells of Christmas cooking reminded him of past Christmastimes when his wife had been alive and his own children little. Now they had gone. His usually cheerful face, with the little laughter wrinkles behind the round steel spectacles, looked sad now. But he went back indoors with a firm step, put up the shutters, and set a pot of coffee to heat on the charcoal stove. Then, with a sigh, he settled in his big armchair.

Papa Panov did not often read, but tonight he pulled down the big old family Bible and, slowly tracing the lines with one finger, he read again the Christmas story. He read how Mary and Joseph, tired by their journey to Bethlehem, found no room for them at the inn, so that Mary's little baby was born in the cowshed.

"Oh dear, oh dear!" exclaimed Papa Panov. "If only they had come here! I would have given them my bed and I could have covered the baby with my patchwork quilt to keep him warm."

He read on about the Wise Men who had come to see the baby Jesus, bringing him splendid gifts. Papa Panov's face fell.

"I have no gift that I could give him," he thought sadly.

Then his face brightened. He put down the Bible, got up, and stretched his long arms to the shelf high up in his little room. He took down a small, dusty box and opened it. Inside was a perfect pair of tiny leather shoes. Papa Panov smiled with satisfaction. Yes, they were as good as he had remembered—the best shoes he had ever made.

"I should give him those," he decided as he gently put them away and sat down again.

He was feeling tired now, and the further he read the sleepier he became. The print began to dance before his eyes so that he closed them, just for a moment. In no time at all Papa Panov was fast asleep.

And as he slept he dreamed. He dreamed that someone was in his room and he knew at once, as one does in dreams, who the person was. It was Jesus.

"You have been wishing that you could see me, Papa Panov," he said kindly. "Then look for me tomorrow. It will be Christmas Day and I will visit you. But look carefully, for I shall not tell you who I am."

When at last Papa Panov awoke, the bells were ringing out and a thin light was filtering through the shutters.

"Bless my soul!" said Papa Panov. "It's Christmas Day!"

He stood up and stretched himself, for he was rather stiff. Then his face filled with happiness as he remembered his dream. This would be a very special Christmas after all, for Jesus was coming to visit. How would he look? Would he be a little baby, as at that first Christmas? Would he be a grown man, a carpenter—or the great King that he is, God's Son? He must watch carefully the whole day through so that he recognized him however he came.

Papa Panov put on a special pot of coffee for his Christmas breakfast, took down the shutters, and looked out of the window. The street was deserted; no one was stirring yet. No one except the road sweeper. He looked as miserable and dirty as ever, and well he might! Whoever wanted to work on Christmas Day—and in the raw cold and bitter freezing mist of such a morning?

Papa Panov opened the shop door, letting

in a thin stream of cold air. "Come in!" he shouted across the street cheerily. "Come and have some hot coffee to keep out the cold!"

The sweeper looked up, scarcely able to believe his ears. He was only too glad to put down his broom and come into the warm room. His old clothes steamed gently in the heat of the stove and he clasped both red hands round the comforting warm mug as he drank.

Papa Panov watched him with satisfaction, but every now and then his eyes strayed to the window. It would never do to miss his special visitor.

"Expecting someone?" the sweeper asked at last. So Papa Panov told him about his dream. "Well, I hope he comes," the sweeper said. "You've given me a bit of Christmas cheer I never expected to have. I'd say you deserve to have your dream come true." And he actually smiled.

When he had gone, Papa Panov put on cabbage soup for his dinner, then went to the door again, scanning the street. He saw no one. But he was mistaken. Someone was coming.

The girl walked so slowly and quietly, hugging the walls of shops and houses, that it was a while before he noticed her. She looked very tired and she was carrying something. As she drew nearer, he could see that it was a baby, wrapped in a thin shawl. There was such sadness in her face and in the pinched little face of the baby that Papa Panov's heart went out to them.

"Won't you come in?" he called, step-ping outside to meet them. "You both need to warm by the fire and rest."

The young mother let him shepherd her indoors and to the comfort of the armchair. She gave a big sigh of relief.

"I'll warm some milk for the baby," Papa Panov said. "I've had children of my own—I can feed her for you." He took the milk from the stove and carefully fed the baby from a spoon, warming her tiny feet by the stove at the same time.

"She needs shoes," the cobbler said.

But the girl replied, "I can't afford shoes; I've got no husband to bring home money. I'm on my way to the next village to get work."

A sudden thought flashed into Papa Panov's mind. He remembered the little shoes he had looked at last night. But he had been keeping those for Jesus. He looked again at the cold little feet and made up his mind.

"Try these on her," he said, handing the baby and the shoes to the mother. The beautiful little shoes were a perfect fit. The girl smiled happily and the baby gurgled with pleasure.

"You have been so kind to us," the girl said, when she got up with her baby to go. "May all your Christmas wishes come true!"

But Papa Panov was beginning to wonder if his very special Christmas wish would come true. Perhaps he had missed his visitor? He looked anxiously up and down the street. There were plenty of people about, but they were all faces that he recognized. There were neighbors going to call on their families.

They nodded and smiled and wished him Happy Christmas! Or beggars—and Papa Panov hurried indoors to fetch them hot soup and a generous hunk of bread, hurrying out again in case he missed the Important Stranger.

All too soon the winter dusk fell. When Papa Panov next went to the door and strained his eyes, he could no longer make out the passersby. Most were home and indoors by now anyway. He walked slowly back into his room at last, put up his shutters and sat down wearily in his armchair.

So it has been just a dream after all.

Jesus had not come.

Then all at once he knew that he was no longer alone in the room.

This was no dream, for he was wide awake. At first he seemed to see before his eyes the long stream of people who had come to him that day. He saw again the old road sweeper, the young mother and her baby, and the beggars he had fed. As they passed, each whispered, "Didn't you see me, Papa Panov?"

"Who are you?" he called out, bewildered.

Then another voice answered him. It was the voice from his dream—the voice of Jesus.

"I was hungry and you fed me," he said. "I was naked and you clothed me. I was cold and you warmed me. I came to you today in every one of those you helped and welcomed."

Then all was quiet and still. Only the sound of the big clock ticking. A great peace and happiness seemed to fill the room, overflowing Papa Panov's heart until he wanted to burst out singing and laughing and dancing with joy.

"So he did come after all!" was all that he said.

Candle for the Christ Child

WILLIAM ARNETTE WOFFORD

This silver candle I shall light
And place upon my windowsill;
Its golden light may help to cheer
Some lone wayfarer on the hill.

It may lead someone to my door,
Someone discouraged down the way,
And I shall bid him come and sup
And share my loaf this Christmas Day.

I cannot give my Lord and King
The gifts Wise Men brought Him of old;
But He will love this candle flame
As much, or more, than costly gold!

And, oh, if this tall candle guides
A beggar who asks warmth and bed,
I shall invite him in, for he
Might be the dear Christ Child instead!

THE JOY OF LOVE

A Christmas Carol

HENRY WADSWORTH LONGFELLOW

I hear along our street
    Pass the minstrel throngs.
Hark! They play so sweet
    On their hautboys Christmas songs.
        Let us by the fire,
        Ever higher,
        Sing them till the night expire.

In December ring
    Every day the chimes;
Loud the glee men sing
    In the street their merry rhymes.
        Let us by the fire,
        Ever higher,
        Sing them till the night expire.

Shepherds at the grange,
    Where the Babe was born,
Sang with many a change
    Christmas carols until morn.

        Let us by the fire,
        Ever higher,
        Sing them till the night expire.

These good people sang
    Songs devout and sweet.
While the rafters rang,
    There they stood with freezing feet.
        Let us by the fire,
        Ever higher,
        Sing them till the night expire.

Who by the fireside stands
    Stamps his feet and sings;
But he who blows his hands,
    Not so gay a carol brings.
        Let us by the fire,
        Ever higher,
        Sing them till the night expire.

Christmas Candle

KAY HOFFMAN

Light a Christmas candle
And let it warmly glow
From out a friendly windowpane
Across new-fallen snow.

Someone lone in passing
Will catch the strong, bright beam
To cheer the rugged path ahead
And set the heart to dream.

Let the warm, glad light-shine
From your own candle's ray
Glow deep within your loving heart
On each and every day.

Light a Christmas candle
To glow within your heart
And touch the life of someone dear
With blessings to impart.

Emerald Punch

In an electric blender, combine one 6-ounce can frozen limeade concentrate, thawed; half the contents of one 12-ounce can frozen lemonade concentrate, thawed; ½ cup sifted powdered sugar; 3½ cups crushed ice; and 2 drops green food coloring. Blend on high speed until slushy. Pour into large heavy-duty plastic freezer bag and freeze. Remove from freezer 30 minutes prior to serving. Place in serving bowl and break into chunks. Add two 2-liter bottles club soda and stir until slushy. Makes twenty 8-ounce servings.

HOT MULLED CIDER

In a large kettle, combine 1 gallon apple cider and 1 cup light brown sugar. In a piece of cheesecloth, place 9 whole cloves, 9 whole allspice, and four 3-inch pieces of stick cinnamon; tie up and place in kettle. Simmer 5 to 10 minutes. Remove spice bag. Pour cider into mugs and add a slice of lemon. Makes sixteen 8-ounce servings.

CHOCOLATE SNOWBALLS

Cream 1¼ cups butter with ⅔ cup granulated sugar until fluffy. Add 1 teaspoon vanilla, 2 cups sifted flour, ⅛ teaspoon salt, ½ cup cocoa, and 2 cups chopped pecans. Mix thoroughly. Refrigerate 3 hours.

Preheat oven to 350°F. Form dough into 1-inch balls, and place on ungreased cookie sheet. Bake 20 minutes. Cool on wire racks; roll in powdered sugar. Makes 6 dozen cookies.

HOLIDAY FRUIT PUNCH

Fill two ice cube trays with cranberry juice and freeze. Empty cranberry ice into punch bowl. Add 8 cups chilled cranberry juice, 3 cups chilled pineapple juice, and 4 cups chilled ginger ale. Mix gently and serve. Garnish glasses with sliced pineapple and oranges, if desired. Makes 16 cups.

A group of carolers sings at the front of the house, their songbooks illuminated by the soft glow of the porch light. The words to "Joy to the World" travel throughout the neighborhood in the cold, crisp night air. Inside the house, hot mulled cider waits to welcome the singers.

Sharing Christmas Love with Others

May the fire of this log warm the cold; may the hungry be fed; may the weary find rest; and may all enjoy Heaven's peace.

—Author Unknown

At Christmas be merry, and thankful withal, And feast thy poor neighbors, the great with the small.

—Thomas Tusser

Christmas is coming;
    The goose is getting fat;
    Please to put a penny
    In the old man's hat;
    If you haven't got a penny,
    A ha'penny will do;
    If you haven't got a ha'penny,
    Then God bless you!

—Beggar's Rhyme

For who hath nought to give but love
    Gives all his heart away
    And giving all, hath all to give
    Another Christmas Day.

—Charles W. Kennedy

A Christmas gift love sends to thee;
    'Tis not a gift that you may see,
    Like frankincense or shining gold,
    Yet 'tis a gift that you may hold.

—Clarence Hawkes

There is love at Christmas because Christmas was born of love. Let us, each one, keep alive this spirit of love and glorify God.

—Josepha Emms

May joy come from God above
To all those who Christmas love.
—THIRTEENTH CENTURY CAROL

SELFISHNESS makes Christmas a burden: love makes it a delight.
—AUTHOR UNKNOWN

BLESSED IS THE SEASON which engages the whole world in a conspiracy of love.
—HAMILTON WRIGHT MABI

Love is a seed, life-bearing, undecayed;
And that immortal germ,
Past bounds of zone and term,
Will grow and cover the whole world with shade.
—BLISS CARMAN

The Christmas Day is dawning;
Our carols now we sing
And pray the coming season
May peace and gladness bring.

To every one, and all of yours,
We wish a merry day
And hope some of its pleasures
Through all the year may stay.
—L. A. FRANCE

SWELL THE NOTES of Christmas song!
Sound it forth through the earth abroad!
—FRANCES RIDLEY HAVERGAL

CHRISTMAS MAY BE a day of feasting, or of prayer, but always it will be a day of remembrance—a day in which we think of everything we have ever loved.
—AUGUSTA E. RUNDEL

IN CHARITY, there is no excess.
—FRANCIS BACON

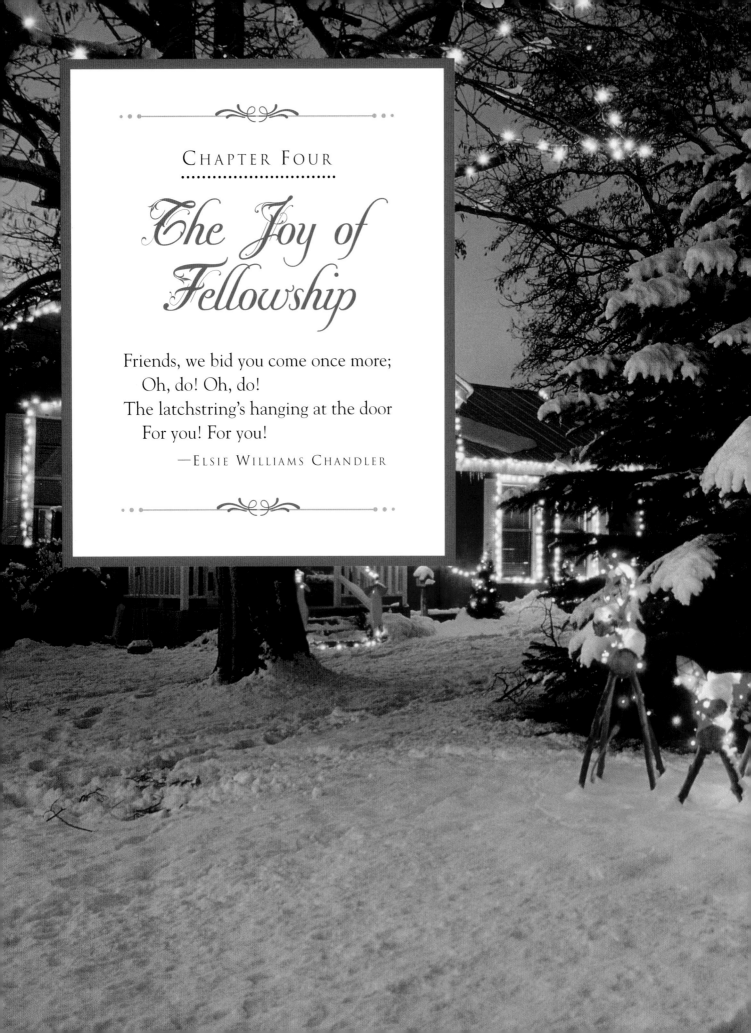

CHAPTER FOUR

The Joy of Fellowship

Friends, we bid you come once more;
Oh, do! Oh, do!
The latchstring's hanging at the door
For you! For you!

—Elsie Williams Chandler

Christmas

AUTHOR UNKNOWN

Ring out, ye joyful Christmas chime,
Glad songs to ev'ry land and clime!
    Nor cease your merry peals until
The message wond'ring shepherds heard
The hearts of all mankind has stirred—
    "Peace on earth; to men goodwill!"

Ring out, ye joyful Christmas bell!
Let ev'ry rich note gladly tell
    That war and blood-lust both shall cease
When men in truth accept the sway
Of Him born on this Christmas Day—
    The manger-cradled Prince of Peace.

Ring out the demons Hate and Might!
Ring in the angels Love and Right!
    Bid Freedom, prostrate on the ground,
Arise and face the golden morn
Whereon the Prince of Peace was born—
    And shout for joy to hear your sound.

Ring out, ye merry Christmas chime,
And usher in the glad New Time
    When, with the royal diadem,
All men have come with joyful sound,
And in true love as King have crowned
    The Blessed Babe of Bethlehem.

Goodwill to Men

DOROTHY BROWN THOMPSON

At Christmas, when old friends are meeting,
We give that long-loved joyous greeting—
    "Merry Christmas!"

While hanging sheaves for winter birds,
Friends in Norway call the words,
    "God Jul!"

With wooden shoes ranged on the hearth,
Dutch celebrators cry their mirth,
    "Vrolijk Kerstfeest!"

In France, that land of courtesy,
Our welcome to our guests would be,
    "Joyeux Noël!"

Enshrining Christmas in her art,
Italy cries from a full heart,
    "Buon Natale!"

When in the land of Christmas trees,
Old Germany, use words like these—
    "Fröhliche Weihnachten!"

Though each land names a different name,
Good will rings through each wish
    the same—
    "Merry Christmas!"

We Wish You a Merry Christmas

TRADITIONAL   TRADITIONAL

At Christmas the Heart Goes Home

Marjorie Holmes

At Christmas all roads lead home.

The filled planes, packed trains, overflowing buses, all speak eloquently of a single destination: home. Despite the crowding and the crushing, the delays, the confusion, we clutch our bright packages and beam our anticipation. We are like birds driven by an instinct we only faintly understand—the hunger to be with our own people.

If we are already snug by our own fireside, surrounded by growing children, or awaiting the return of older ones who are away, then the heart takes a side trip. In memory we journey back to the Christmases of long ago. Once again we are curled into quivering balls of excitement, listening to the mysterious rustle of tissue paper and the tinkle of untold treasures as parents perform their magic on Christmas Eve. Or we recall the special Christmases that are like little landmarks in the life of a family.

One memory is particularly dear to me—a Christmas during the Great Depression. My sister Gwen and her schoolteacher husband, on his first job in another state, were expecting their first baby. My brother Harold, an aspiring actor, was traveling with a road show. I was a senior working my way through a small college five hundred miles away. My boss had offered me fifty dollars—a fortune!—just to keep the office open the two weeks he and his wife would be gone.

"And boy, do I need the money. Mom, I know you'll understand," I wrote.

I wasn't prepared for her brave if wistful reply. The other kids couldn't make it either. Except for my kid brother Barney, she and Dad would be alone. "This house is going to seem empty, but don't worry—we'll be okay."

I did worry, though. Our first Christmas apart! And as the carols drifted up the stairs, as the corridors rang with the laughter and chatter of other girls packing up to leave, my misery deepened.

Then one night when the dorm was almost empty, I had a long-distance call. "Gwen!" I gasped. "What's wrong?" (Long distance usually meant an emergency in those days.)

"Listen, Leon's got a new generator, and we think the old jalopy can make it home.

I've wired Harold—if he can meet us halfway, he can ride with us. But don't tell the folks; we want to surprise them. Marj, you've just got to come too."

"But I haven't got a dime for presents."

"Neither have we. Cut up a catalog and bring pictures of all the goodies you'd buy if you could—and will someday!"

"I could do that, Gwen. But I just can't leave here now."

When we hung up I reached for the scissors. Furs and perfume. Wristwatches, clothes, cars—how all of us longed to lavish beautiful things on those we loved. Well, at least I could mail mine home—with IOUs.

I was still dreaming over this "wish list" when I was called to the phone again. It was the boss, saying he'd decided to close the office after all. My heart leaped up, for if it wasn't too late to catch a ride as far as Fort Dodge with the girl down the hall . . . ! I ran to pound on her door.

They already had a load, she said—but if I was willing to sit on somebody's lap . . . her dad was downstairs waiting. I threw things into a suitcase, then rammed a hand down the torn lining of my coat sleeve so fast it emerged mittened and I had to start over.

It was snowing as we piled into that heaterless car. We drove all night with the side curtains flapping, singing and hugging each other to keep warm. Not minding—how could we? We were going home!

"Marj!" Mother stood at the door, clutching her robe about her, silver-black

hair spilling down her back, eyes large with alarm, then incredulous joy. "Oh . . . Marj."

I'll never forget those eyes or the feel of her arms around me, so soft and warm after the bitter cold. My feet felt frozen after that all-night drive, but they warmed up as my parents fed me and put me to bed. And when I woke up hours later, it was to the jangle of the sleigh bells Dad hung on the door each year. And voices. My kid brother shouting, "Harold! Gwen!" The clamor of astonished greetings, the laughter, the kissing, the questions. And we all gathered around the kitchen table the way we used to, recounting our adventures.

"I had to hitchhike clear to Peoria," my older brother scolded merrily. "Me, the leading man. . . ." He lifted an elegant two-toned shoe—with a flapping sole—"In these!"

"But by golly, you got here." Dad's chubby face was beaming. Then suddenly he broke down—Dad, who never cried. "We're together!"

Together. The best present we could give one another, we realized. All of us. Just being here in the old house where we'd shared so many Christmases. No gift on our lavish lists, if they could materialize, could equal that. . . .

In most Christmases since that memorable one we've been lucky. During the years our children were growing up there were no separations. Then one year, appallingly, history repeated itself. For valid reasons, not a single faraway child could get home. Worse,

my husband had flown to Florida for some vital surgery. A proud, brave man—he was adamant about our not coming with him "just because it's Christmas," when he'd be back in another week.

Like my mother before me, I still had one lone chick left—Melanie, fourteen. "We'll get along fine," she said, trying to cheer me.

We built a big fire every evening, went to church, wrapped presents, pretended. But the ache in our hearts kept swelling. And the day before Christmas we burst into mutual tears. "Mommy, it's just not right for Daddy to be down there alone!"

"I know it." Praying for a miracle, I ran to the telephone. The airlines were hopeless, but there was one roomette available on the last train to Miami. Almost hysterical with relief, we threw things into bags.

And what a Christmas Eve! Excited as conspirators, we cuddled together in that cozy space. Melanie hung a tiny wreath in the window, and we settled down to watch the endless pageantry flashing by to the rhythmic clicking song of the rails. . . . Little villages and city streets—all dancing with lights and decorations and sparkling Christmas trees. . . . And cars and snowy countrysides and people—all the people. Each one on his or her special pilgrimage of love and celebration this precious night.

At last we drifted off to sleep. But hours later I awoke to a strange stillness. The train had stopped. And, raising the shade, I peered out on a very small town. Silent, deserted, with only a few lights still burning. And under the bare branches, along a lonely street, a figure was walking. A young man in sailor blues, head bent, hunched under the weight of the sea bag on his shoulders, and I thought—*Home! Poor kid, he's almost home.* And I wondered if there was someone still up waiting for him; or if anyone knew he was coming at all. And my heart cried out to him, for he was suddenly my own son—and my own ghost, and the soul of us all—driven, so immutably driven by this annual call, "Come home!"

Home for Christmas. There must be some deep psychological reason why we turn so instinctively toward home at this special time. Perhaps we are acting out the ancient story of a man and a woman and a coming child, plodding along with their donkey toward their destination. It was necessary for Joseph, the earthly father, to go home to be taxed. Each male had to return to the city of his birth.

Birth. The tremendous miracle of birth shines through every step and syllable of the Bible story. The long, arduous trip across the mountains of Galilee and Judea was also the journey of a life toward birth. Mary was already in labor when they arrived in Bethlehem, so near the time of her delivery that in desperation, since the inn was full, her husband settled for a humble stable.

The child who was born on that first Christmas grew up to be a man. Jesus. He healed many people, taught us many impor-

tant things. But the message that has left the most lasting impression and given the most hope and comfort is this: that we do have a home to go to, and there will be an ultimate homecoming. A place where we will indeed be reunited with those we love.

Anyway, that's my idea of heaven. A place where Mother is standing in the door, probably bossing Dad the way she used to about the turkey or the tree, and he's enjoying every minute of it. And old friends and neighbors are streaming in and out and the sense of love and joy and celebration will go on forever.

A place where every day will be Christmas, with everybody there together. At home.

Invitation at Christmas

CATHERINE ECKRICH

We have placed a candle in our window:
May its warmth and glow reach out to
    where you are!
Our hearts and house are lighted for
    your coming.
Atop our tree now shines the Christmas star.

Now at this wondrous summit of the season,
Where again the miracle of Christmas towers,
May our love and welcome light your pathway,
You and yours, to us and ours!

Gathering with Loved Ones at Christmas

Sing hey for the chimney and rooftree wide,
Sing hey for the walls and the floor,
For the warmth of the fire on the glowing hearth,
And the welcoming open door,
But most of all for the peace and goodwill
And the joy at our deep heart's core.

—ELIZABETH GOUDGE

Among the many gifts life sends,
None are more dear than loyal friends;
That's why no words can quite express
The many ways in which you bless.

May Christmas be a happy day,
Bringing all its gifts your way;
And when we reach another year,
May passing moments offer cheer.

—BEATRICE BRANCH

A merry Christmas to you—
A Christmas bright and sweet,
With fun and lovingkindness
And many a charming treat;
Of Christmas gifts most new and rare
May you have a goodly share.

—AUTHOR UNKNOWN

Your friendship is a glowing ember
Through the year; and each December
From its warm and living spark
We kindle flame against the dark
And with its shining radiance light
Our tree of faith on Christmas night.

—THELMA J. LUND

I HAVE ALWAYS thought of Christmas as a good time; a kind, forgiving, generous, pleasant time; a time when men and women seem to open their hearts freely, and so I say, God bless Christmas!

—CHARLES DICKENS

It DIDN'T SURPRISE me to learn that Americans send out a billion and a half Christmas cards every year. . . . We are a genial race, as neighborly abroad as at home, fond of perpetuating the chance encounter, the golden hour, the unique experience. . . .

—JAMES THURBER

I salute you! There is nothing I can give
   you which you have not; but there is much
   that, while I cannot give, you can take.
No heaven can come to us unless our hearts
   find rest in it today. Take Heaven.
No peace lies in the future which is not hidden
   in this present instant. Take Peace.
The gloom of the world is but a shadow;
   behind it, yet within our reach, is joy.
   Take Joy.
And so, at this Christmastime, I greet you,
   with the prayer that for you, now and
   forever, the day breaks and the shadows
   flee away.

—FRA GIOVANNI

Sing hey! Sing hey!
   For Christmas Day;
   Twine mistletoe and holly,
   For friendship glows
   In winter snows,
   And so let's all be jolly.

—AUTHOR UNKNOWN

I heard the bells on Christmas Day
   Their old, familiar carols play;
   And wild and sweet the words repeat
   Of peace on earth, goodwill to men.

—HENRY WADSWORTH LONGFELLOW

CHRISTMAS IS THE season for kindling the fire of hospitality in the hall, the genial flame of charity in the heart.

—WASHINGTON IRVING

What Is Christmas?

GOLDIE WILLIAMS

It's not the lights or mistletoe
Or gifts we give with cheer:
Our Christmastime is not complete
Unless our friends are near.

It's not the "Merry Christmas" voiced,
But love within the heart,
The memories of the ones who are
So much of us a part.

The spirit of this blessed day
I only can express
By wishing all dear friends of ours
Peace, joy, and happiness.

Candlelit Heart

MARY E. LINTON

Somewhere across the winter world tonight
You will be hearing chimes that fill the air;
Christmas extends its all-enfolding light
Across the distance . . . something we can share.
You will be singing, just the same as I,
These old familiar songs we know so well,
And you will see these same stars in your sky
And wish upon that brightest one that fell.
I shall remember you and trim my tree,
One shining star upon the topmost bough;
I will hang wreaths of faith that all may see.
Tonight I glimpse beyond the here and now;
And all the years that we must be apart,
I keep a candle lighted in my heart.

The Christmas Latchstring

GEORGIA B. ADAMS

Stop by our home, the latchstring's out;
Enjoy our Christmastime.
The holly's up, the tree is dressed
In ornaments sublime.

The homemade taffy's on the shelf,
The home-baked cookies, too,
Are on the dining-room table,
And home-popped popcorn too.

The hand-wound phonograph is set
To play some carols sweet;
The player piano's ready too—
What fun for nimble feet!

Just stop by any time at all,
A welcome waits for you;
Enjoy our Christmas with us, friend.
Now come on in, please do!

SPICE BITES

In a medium bowl, cut ½ cup softened butter and the contents of one 5-ounce jar old English Cheddar cheese spread into 1 cup all-purpose flour. Stir in 2 tablespoons water; shape mixture into a ball. Refrigerate overnight.

Preheat oven to 375°F. Roll out dough to a scant ¼-inch thickness and cut out 2-inch rounds with a drinking glass or biscuit cutter dipped in flour. Spoon ½ teaspoon hot-pepper jelly onto the center of each round; fold dough in half over the filling and crimp edges together with a fork. Bake 10 minutes or until golden brown. Makes 2 to 3 dozen turnovers.

SUGARED PECANS

In a medium saucepan, combine 1½ cups granulated sugar and ½ cup orange juice; boil to soft-ball stage, 236°F. Remove from heat and add 1 teaspoon grated orange peel and 3 cups pecan halves. Stir until pecan halves are well coated. Spread onto wax paper and carefully separate pecans; allow to cool. Makes 6 to 8 servings.

PASTRY PACKAGES

Preheat oven to 375°F. In a small bowl, combine 1 cup shredded Cheddar cheese and ¼ cup thinly sliced green onion; set aside. Separate dough from two 8-ounce cans refrigerated crescent dinner rolls into 16 triangles. Cut each triangle in half from a long side to the opposite corner to make 32 triangles. Drop a rounded teaspoon of cheese-onion mixture in the middle of each triangle. Fold all three corners to the center of each triangle, over-lapping the points and pressing the ends together to seal each bundle. Place on ungreased cookie sheet and brush each bundle lightly with melted butter. Lightly sprinkle dried dill weed over the pastries. Bake 10 to 13 minutes or until golden brown; serve warm. Makes 32 mini-pastries.

The logs in the fireplace crackle as they burn, their burnished light reflected in the faces of gathering family and friends. Holding steaming mugs of cocoa, the visitors warm their backs in front of the hearth and listen to the carols that play on the radio. The scent from a cinnamon candle swirls throughout the room as golden snacks emerge from the oven.

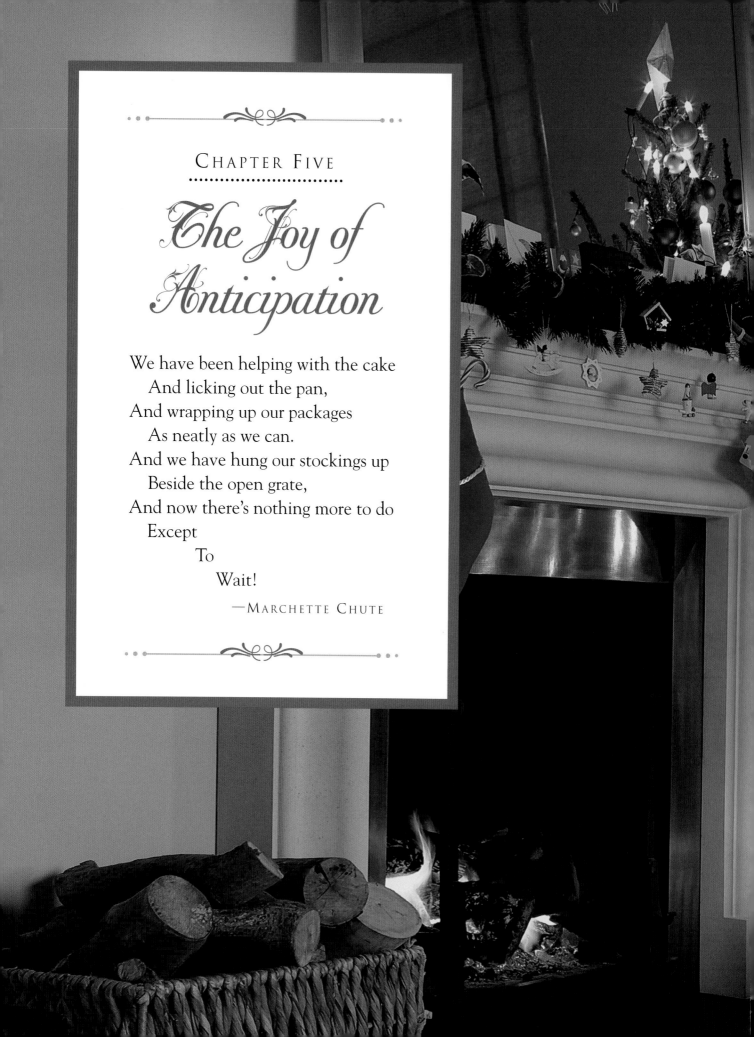

CHAPTER FIVE

The Joy of Anticipation

We have been helping with the cake
  And licking out the pan,
And wrapping up our packages
  As neatly as we can.
And we have hung our stockings up
  Beside the open grate,
And now there's nothing more to do
  Except
        To
          Wait!

—MARCHETTE CHUTE

YES, VIRGINIA, THERE IS A SANTA CLAUS

Francis P. Church

The *New York Sun*
September 21, 1897
We take pleasure in answering thus prominently the com-munication below, expressing at the same time our great gratification that its faithful author is numbered among the friends of the *Sun*:

Dear Editor:

I am eight years old.

Some of my little friends say there is no Santa Claus.

Papa says, "If you see it in the *Sun*, it's so."

Please tell me the truth, is there a Santa Claus?

Virginia O'Hanlon
115 West 95th Street

Virginia, your little friends are wrong. They have been affected by the skepticism of a skeptical age. They do not believe except what they see. They think that nothing can be which is not comprehensible by their little minds. All minds, Virginia, whether they be men's or children's, are little. In this great universe of ours, man is a mere insect, an ant, in his intellect, as compared with the boundless world about him, as measured by the intelligence capable of grasping the whole of truth and knowledge.

Yes, Virginia, there is a Santa Claus. He exists as certainly as love and generosity and devotion exist, and you know that they abound and give to your life its highest beauty and joy. Alas! how dreary would be the world if there were no Santa Claus! It would be as dreary as if there were no Virginias. There would be no childlike faith then, no poetry, no romance to make tolerable this existence. We should have no enjoyment, except in sense and sight. The external light with which childhood fills the world would be extinguished.

Not believe in Santa Claus! You might as well not believe in fairies. You might get your papa to hire men to watch in all the chimneys on Christmas Eve to catch Santa Claus, but even if you did not see Santa Claus coming down, what would that prove? Nobody sees Santa Claus, but that is no sign that there is no Santa Claus. The most real things in the world are those that neither children nor men can see. Did you ever see fairies dancing on the lawn? Of course not, but that's no proof that they are not there. Nobody can conceive or imagine all the wonders there are unseen and unseeable in the world.

You tear apart the baby's rattle and see what makes the noise inside, but there is a veil covering the unseen world which not the strongest man, nor even the united strength of all the strongest men that ever lived could tear apart. Only faith, fancy, poetry, love, romance, can push aside that curtain and view and picture the supernal beauty and glory beyond. Is it all real? Ah, Virginia, in all this world there is nothing else real and abiding.

No Santa Claus! Thank God he lives, and he lives forever. A thousand years from now, Virginia, nay, ten times ten thousand years from now, he will continue to make glad the heart of childhood.

Christmas in the Heart

AUTHOR UNKNOWN

It is Christmas in the mansion,
Yule-log fires and silken frocks.
It is Christmas in the cottage;
Mother's filling little socks.

It is Christmas on the highway,
In the thronging, busy mart;
But the dearest, truest Christmas
Is the Christmas in the heart.

The Week Before Christmas

AUTHOR UNKNOWN

'Tis the week before Christmas and every night
As soon as the children are snuggled up tight
And have sleepily murmured their wishes and prayers,
Such fun as goes on in the parlor downstairs!
For Father, Big Brother, and Grandfather, too,
Start in with great vigor their youth to renew.
The grown-ups are having great fun—all is well;
And they play till it's long past their hour for bed.

They try to solve puzzles and each one enjoys
The magical thrill of mechanical toys.
Even Mother must play with a doll that can talk;
And if you assist it, it's able to walk.
It's really no matter if paint may be scratched,
Or a cogwheel, a nut, or a bolt gets detached;
The grown-ups are having great fun—all is well;
The children don't know it, and Santa won't tell.

CHRISTMAS EVE

Dorothy Brown Thompson

t is Christmas Eve—the festival that belongs to mothers
and fathers and children, all
over the world. It's not a time to
talk about situations, or conditions,
or reactions, or people who emerge
briefly into the news. My seven-year-
old son asked me this evening to tell
him what Christmas was like when I
was a little girl, before people came

home for Christmas in airplanes, thirty-odd years ago. And so I told him this:

A long, long time ago, when your mother was your age, and not nearly as tall as you, she lived with her mother, and father, and younger brother, and little sister, in a Methodist parsonage, in Hamburg, New York. It was a tall wooden house, with a narrow veranda on the side, edged with curlicues of woodwork at the top, and it looked across a lawn at the church where Father preached every Sunday morning and evening. In the backyard there were old Baldwin and Greening apple trees, and a wonderful, wonderful barn. But that is another story. The village now has turned into a suburb of the neighboring city of Buffalo, and fathers who work there go in and out every day on the trains and buses, but then it was just a little country town, supported by the surrounding farms.

For weeks before Christmas we were very, very busy. Mother was busy in the kitchen cutting up citron and sorting out raisins and clarifying suet for the Christmas pudding—and shooing all of us out of the room, when we crept in to snatch a raisin or a bit of kernel from the butternuts that my little brother set to cracking on the woodshed floor, with an old-fashioned flatiron.

I would lock myself into my little bedroom to bend over a handkerchief that I was hemstitching for my mother. It is very hard to hemstitch when you are seven years old, and the thread would knot, and break, and then one would have to begin again, with a little rough place, where one had started over. I'm afraid the border of that handkerchief was just one succession of knots and starts.

The homemade presents were only a tiny part of the work. There was the Christmas tree! Mr. Heist, from my father's Armor parish, had brought it in from his farm, a magnificent hemlock that touched the ceiling. We were transported with admiration, but what a tree to trim! For there was no money to buy miles of tinsel and boxes of colored glass balls.

But in the pantry was a huge stone jar of popcorn. When school was over, in the afternoons, we all gathered in the back parlor, which was the family sitting room. The front parlor was a cold place, where portraits of John Wesley and Frances Willard hung on the walls, and their eyes, I remember, would follow a naughty child accusingly around the room. The sofas in that room were of walnut, with roses and grapes carved on their backs, just where they'd stick into your back, if you fidgeted in them, and were covered with horsehair which was slippery when it was new, and tickly when it was old. But that room was given over to visits from the local tycoons who sometimes contributed to the church funds, and couples who came to be married.

The back parlor was quite, quite different. It had an ingrain carpet on the floor, with patterns of maple leaves, white muslin curtains at the windows, and an assortment of

chairs contributed by the Parsonage committee. A Morris chair, I remember, and some rockers, and a fascinating cabinet which was a desk and a bookcase, and a chest of drawers, and a mirror, all in one.

In this room there was a round iron stove, a very jolly stove, a cozy stove that winked at you with its red isinglass eyes. On top of this stove was a round iron plate; it was flat, and a wonderful place to pop corn. There was a great copper kettle, used for making maple syrup, and we shook the popper on the top of the stove—first I shook, until my arm was tired, and then Willard shook, until he was tired, and even the baby shook. The corn popped, and we poured it into the kettle and emptied the kettle, and poured it full again, until there was a whole barrelful of popcorn, as white and fluffy as the snow that carpeted the lawn between the parsonage and the church.

Then we got a darning needle, a big one, and a ball of string. We strung the popcorn into long, long ropes, to hang upon the tree. But that was only half of it! There were stars to be cut out of kindergarten paper—red, and green, and silver, and gold—and walnuts to be wrapped in gold paper, or painted with gold paint out of the paintbox that I had been given for my birthday. One got the paint into one's fingernails, and it smelled like bananas. And red apples to be polished, because a shiny apple makes a brave show on a tree. And when it was all finished, it was Christmas Eve.

For Christmas Eve we all wore our best clothes. Baby in a little challis dress as blue as her eyes, and I had a new pinafore of Swiss lawn that my Aunt Margaret had sent me from England. We waited, breathless, in the front parlor while the candles were lit.

Then my mother sat at the upright piano in a rose-red cashmere dress and played; and my father sang, in his lovely, pure, gay, tenor voice:

> It came upon a midnight clear
> That glorious song of old,
> From angels bending near the earth
> To touch their harps of gold.

And then we all marched in. It is true that we had decorated the tree ourselves, and knew intimately everything on it, but it shone in the dark room like an angel, and I could see the angels bending down, and it was so beautiful that one could hardly bear it. We all cried, "Merry Christmas!" and kissed one another.

There were bundles under the tree, most alluring bundles! But they didn't belong to Christmas Eve. They were for the morning. Before the morning came, three little children would sit sleepily in the pews of their father's church and hear words drowsily, and shift impatiently, and want to go to sleep in order to wake up very, very, early!

Silver Bells

Jay Livingston

Ray Evans

smile, and on ev'ry street cor-ner you hear:

Silver bells,   silver bells;
Ring-a-ling,   hear them ring;

it's Christmas - time in the cit - y.

Soon it will be Christmas Day.

THE TOUCH
OF ANGEL'S WINGS

Idella Bodie

It was Christmas Eve. Elizabeth sat on the edge of her little daughter's bed. She bent over and kissed the rose-petaled cheek. With golden-flax hair spreading over the pillow and long lashes heavy with sleep, Marya looked for all the world like an angel.

Elizabeth's heart swelled with love and overflowed with the sweet joy of sharing. On this, the holiest night, she had told her little daughter about the visit of the angel.

The two of them had sat listening to the delicate Swedish chimes and watching the little angels dance round and round above the glow of magical candles. The first Christmas after Marya was born, Elizabeth's mother had given her the family keepsake. "Because you always loved it so," her mother had said.

Earlier, as Elizabeth saw the glow of candles reflected in her little daughter's blue eyes, she felt the tender excitement mounting until the two of them and the candles were one. And Elizabeth knew it was time to share her marvelous secret.

With joy swelling even greater, Elizabeth remembered the first Christmas the angel had given her the joy of the Christmas season.

She was about Marya's age the evening she sat at the table long after the dishes had been cleared away. With her chin cupped in her hands, she followed the movement of the angels and the light tinkling of the chimes.

"Elizabeth is enchanted by those angel chimes," her mother announced to no one in particular.

It was that night Elizabeth was awakened by the soft whir.

Moonlight shimmered through the curtains of her bedroom window like the lace on her grandmother's dresses. Elizabeth lay very still. Then in the soft darkness she saw the angel—one of them from the chimes—moving around her room. Moonlight frosted the tips of the angel's wings, and the tiny horn by her mouth made the softest of sounds like twinkling bits of laughter.

Suddenly a silver magic enveloped the room, making Elizabeth's heart tremble. But she was not afraid. Under covers streaked by moonlight, she marveled at the angel's fluttering. She saw the gossamer wings brush the dolls on the trunk against the wall, her dollhouse, the edges of her storybooks, her clothes. And with the touch the whole room became a place of heavenly sweetness.

And then, as quietly as the enchantment had come, it disappeared. The whirring stopped and the angel was gone. Yet a glory shone over the room until Elizabeth fell asleep again.

The next morning, it was if the angel's wings had cleansed and blessed the world. How new everything looked! The faces of her dolls were clear and bright. Even the air smelled clean. It was as if Elizabeth was seeing and feeling everything for the first time. Her whole world was different—it had been touched by the angel's wings.

Eager to share, she had burst into the kitchen where her parents and brothers had already gathered around the breakfast table.

"Last night," she began, pointing to the little angels standing frozen in their angelic poses, "one of the angels came to my room and—"

"Yeah, Elizabeth—" Her brothers' laughter cut across her beautiful story.

"Boys!" her mother reprimanded. "Elizabeth has a vivid imagination." And Elizabeth thought she detected a trace of a smile at the corner of her father's mouth.

Even so, the angel's touch filled the Christmas season with wonder and magic. On other Christmases the angel's coming was never quite the same. Once or twice she thought she heard the whirring or the faint tooting of the horn. Another time she saw the moonlight frosting gossamer wings in flight. But Elizabeth knew the little angel always came and that the coming gave the world a special glow of miracles.

And tonight, after carrying this beautiful secret in her heart for all these years, she had shared it with her very own little girl. Now the beauty and magic of the angel's touch would live forever as it passed from heart to heart in love.

Those without faith might say it was just a dream, but Elizabeth knew that she had been chosen by God to be blessed with the gift of the angel's visit. For only those who believe can know the touch of the angel's wings and the miracles it brings. For in them Christ is born again each Christmas.

Perhaps tonight Marya would be awakened by the soft whir of wings.

Carol of Christmas

NANCY BYRD TURNER

Day fades across the winter world;
   The snow is cold and deep;
Beside the window, Christmas Eve
   Our twilight watch we keep.

O Christmas stars, O Christmas stars,
   Before our earnest eyes,
You write the sweetest tale of earth
   Across the Christmas skies!

The wind drops down, the fields are still,
   The air is hushed and clear;
Far music trembles up the hill
   Upon our listening ear.

O Christmas bells, O Christmas bells,
   Ring silvery and long
Unto our little hearts you see
   The Christmas angels' song!

The Magic of the Coming Day

At Christmas, play and make good cheer,
For Christmas comes but once a year.
—Thomas Tusser

If you've lost your zest for Christmas,
    Lost your love for all its cheer;
If you scoff at gifts and giving
    As the Christmastime draws near,
If you frown at all the clatter
    When old Santa trims his tree,
Tell me, please, what is the matter?
    Something's wrong, it seems to me!
—Lurana Sheldon

A tall red taper burns below
    A holly wreath. The crystal snow
Flings back the sliver light
Of stars. Still is the night . . .
And all the world recalls a birth,
An angel's song, and peace on earth.
—Virginia Blanck Moore

Villagers all, this frosty tide,
    Let your doors swing open wide;

Though wind may follow and snow betide,
Yet draw us in by your fire to bide:

Joy shall be yours in the morning.
—Kenneth Grahame

How can you tell when it's Christmastime? Look into a child's shining eyes—you'll see Christmas there. See a neighbor's wave, hear his cheerful greeting—you'll know Christmas is near.

—Author Unknown

I'll hang up my stocking to hold what he brings;
I hope he will fill it with lots of nice things:
He must know how dearly I love sugarplums;
I'd like a big box when Santa Claus comes.

—ELIZABETH SILE

CHRISTMAS IS not a date.

It is a state of mind.

—MARY ELLEN CHASE

How many days to Christmas?
Forty, thirty, and then—
Twenty-five, twenty, seventeen,
Fourteen, eleven, ten.

Nine, eight, seven—six, five, four—
Three days, two days, slowly go.
But the last day before Christmas
Is—slow—slow—slow.

—JAMES S. TIPPETT

The time draws near the birth of Christ:
The moon is hid; the night is still;
The Christmas bells from hill to hill
Answer each other in the midst.

—ALFRED, LORD TENNYSON

December, month of holly,
    pine, and balsam,
Of berries red, of candles'
    mellow light,
Of home and fireside,
    laughter, happy faces,
Of peace that comes upon
    the holy night.

—AUTHOR UNKNOWN

Hang up the baby's stocking:
    Be sure you don't forget;
The dear little dimpled darling,
    She ne'er saw Christmas yet;

But I've told her all about it,
    And she opened her big eyes,
And I'm sure she understood it—
    She looked so funny and so wise.

—AUTHOR UNKNOWN

DELIGHTS FOR THE CHRISTMAS EVE SUPPER

ORANGE, WALNUT, AND CRANBERRY SALAD

Preheat oven to 325°F. In a large bowl, combine ¾ teaspoon allspice, ½ teaspoon salt, and ¼ teaspoon ground ginger. Stir in 1½ tablespoons water and 6 tablespoons honey. Add 1 cup walnut pieces; toss to coat. Strain nuts, reserving liquid and spreading nuts on a baking sheet lined with parchment paper . Sprinkle nuts with 2 teaspoons sugar. Bake until golden brown, about 17 minutes. Cool completely.

In a medium saucepan, combine ¾ cup water, ¾ cup cranberry juice cocktail, and reserved liquid. Stir in ½ cup dried cranberries. Bring to a boil; reduce heat to medium-low and simmer until cranberries soften and liquid is reduced to a thin syrup, about 20 minutes. Remove from heat and cool completely.

Peel 8 oranges and slice into ½-inch thick rounds. Arrange slices on a serving platter. Spoon cranberry mixture over orange slices and top with nuts. Garnish with fresh mint sprigs, if desired. Makes 8 servings.

CARAMELIZED CHESTNUTS AND BRUSSELS SPROUTS

Preheat oven to 350°F. Using a paring knife, cut a large "x" into the shell of each of ¾ pound fresh chestnuts. Arrange on a baking pan in a single layer, cut side up. Roast until flesh is tender, 20 to 25 minutes. Remove from oven; immediately remove and discard shells, keeping chestnuts whole if possible. Set aside. In a large sauté pan over medium-high heat, melt 2 tablespoons unsalted butter and 1 tablespoon olive oil. Add 2 pounds Brussels sprouts; season with salt and pepper. Cook, stirring occasionally, until golden, 16 to 18 minutes. Add roasted chestnuts and cook, stirring occasionally, until Brussels sprouts are tender and spotted deep brown, 20 to 25 minutes. Add ½ cup cider vinegar, ¼ cup sugar, and ¼ cup low-sodium canned turkey stock, skimmed of fat; cook, stirring occasionally, until reduced to a syrup, 4 to 5 minutes. Transfer to a serving dish. Makes 8 servings.

HONEY-GLAZED MEATBALLS

Preheat oven to 350°F. In a small saucepan, combine 1 tablespoon all-purpose flour and ¼ cup orange juice. Gradually stir in 1 additional cup orange juice, 1½ teaspoons lemon juice, and ¼ cup honey. Bring to a boil, stirring constantly. Remove from heat; set aside. In a large bowl, combine ¼ cup finely chopped onion, 1 pound lean ground beef, ¾ cup fresh bread crumbs, 1 egg, 1 teaspoon salt, and ¼ teaspoon pepper; mix well. Shape into 1-inch meatballs and place on a 10- x 15-inch baking pan. Brush honey glaze on meatballs. Bake meatballs 25 minutes or until brown, brushing twice during baking with remaining glaze. Remove to serving platter and garnish with orange slices; serve warm. Makes 2 dozen meatballs.

Above the flames of the tiny candles, the brass angel chimes spin in the center of the coffee table. From the Christmas tree in front of the window drifts the fragrance of fresh pine. As a simple supper warms in the kitchen, children and adults gather on the sofas and chairs for the annual reading of "The Night Before Christmas."

Christmas Is Coming

HARRIET WHIPPLE

We're seeing manger scenes about
And hearing carols once more;
Christmas is coming nearer now,
And Santa is in each store.
They're selling trees of evergreen
To trim with glowing lights.
Counters are laden high with toys
In which each child delights.

There are candles in the windows
And wreaths upon each door
With mistletoe and holly
Just where they were before.
Closets are full of packages
All wrapped and marked with care,
And in many secret places
Gifts are hidden here and there.

Each kitchen's now a busy place
And smells extremely nice
As the cookies, pies, and fruitcakes
Send forth the scents of spice.
There are smiles on all the faces
Of shoppers that we meet,
For there is Christmas spirit
In everyone we greet.

Cards come in with every mail
And Santa socks appear;
Children count remaining days
Till Christmas day is here.
We're hoping for a bit of snow
To make a festive scene,
For Christmas isn't quite as bright
If the outdoor world is green.

A Real Santa Claus

FRANK DEMPSTER SHERMAN

Santa Claus, I hang for you,
By the mantel, stockings two:
One for me and one to go
To another boy I know.

There's a chimney in the town
You have never traveled down.
Should you chance to enter there
You would find a room all bare:
Not a stocking could you spy,
Matters not how you might try;
And the shoes you'd find are such

As no boy would care for much.
In a broken bed you'd see
Someone just about like me,
Dreaming of the pretty toys,
Which you bring to other boys,
And to him a Christmas seems
Merry only in his dreams.

All he dreams then, Santa Claus,
Stuff the stocking with, because
When it's filled up to the brim
I'll be Santa Claus to him!

CHAPTER SIX

The Joy of Celebration

Then be ye glad, good people,
This night of all the year.
And light ye up your candles,
For His star, it shineth clear.

—AUTHOR UNKNOWN

The Christmas Fires

ANNE P. L. FIELD

The Christmas fires brightly gleam
    And dance among the holly boughs,
The Christmas pudding's spicy steam
    With fragrance fills the house,
While merry grows each friendly soul
Over the foaming wassail bowl.

Resplendent stands the glitt'ring tree,
    Weighted with gifts for old and young,
The children's faces shine with glee
    And joyous is each tongue,
While lads and lassies come and go
Under the festive mistletoe.

When suddenly the frosty air
    Is filled with music, voices sweet,
Lo! see the Christmas waits are there,
    Snow-crowned and bare of feet;
Yet high and clear their voices ring,
And glad their Christmas caroling:

O Child of Mary's tender care!
O little Child so pure and fair!
Cradled within the manger hay
On that divine first Christmas Day!
The hopes of every age and race
Are centered in Thy radiant face!

O Child whose glory fills the earth!
O little Child of lowly birth!
The shepherds, guided from afar,
Stood worshiping beneath the star,
And Wise Men fell on bended knee
And homage offered unto Thee!

Joy to the World

Isaac Watts

Lowell Mason

Joy to the world! The Lord has come: let

earth re - ceive her King. Let

ev' - ry heart pre-

CHRISTMAS AT OUR HOUSE

Ruth Bell Graham

and Gigi Graham Tchividjian

D o you ever have oysters for breakfast?

We do, once a year, on Christmas morning.

Perhaps you wonder why we have them then. When I go to the grocery store the day before Christmas and ask for oysters, I like to tell the man when I'm going to serve them.

"Oysters for breakfast!" he says, and he is very puzzled. Then I explain that my mother always served oyster stew for Christmas breakfast when I was a girl in China. It was a family custom. And when my father, who is a doctor, decided that it was time to bring his family back to America, we brought back the custom of oysters for Christmas breakfast too.

Let's say that it's Christmas morning. The tree is over there by the window, with the presents beneath it and its branches loaded down with warm-colored lights, candy canes, ornaments, and the smallest gifts. And here in front of the enormous fireplace—big enough to stand up in, when there's no fire—are the stockings, one for every child and cousin. The presents have to wait until after breakfast, but the stockings are for now.

After the stockings come breakfast, and you know what is on the table today, don't you? Oysters, floating in a big, steaming stew. (Want to know a secret? Personally, I don't like oysters for breakfast. I never did, not even when I was a girl back in China. But the stew part is fine.)

Our children think breakfast takes forever on Christmas morning. Never do the grown-ups eat so much. They sit around and drink cup after cup of coffee, and they lean back and talk about how long it's been since they were all together, and they even waste precious minutes looking out over the valley and saying what a lovely day it is. But then comes the wonderful moment when finally they're through, and they get up, scraping their chairs on the floor, and

everyone goes back into the living room to open the presents.

It takes a long time because everyone wants to see what everyone else has received. But finally the very last package is opened. The floor is a heap of paper and ribbons and the grown-ups are saying, as they did last year, that there's really too much and that next year they will have to buy fewer presents.

And now comes the moment that's really Christmas. The fire is snapping. Christmas music is playing softly on the record player. Everyone makes himself comfortable, some on the floor, some in chairs, some on the window seat. It's time for the Christmas story. Father opens the Bible to the second chapter of the book of Luke. When he begins to read, the room is suddenly still with a special stillness that it has only at this time on Christmas morning. We are very quiet as we listen again to the wonderful story.

[Gigi, Ruth's eldest daughter, tells this story of her son's reaction to the family traditions.]

Christmas arrived with all the joy, excitement, and anticipation that usually accompanies this happy holiday. Our children had been making endless lists for weeks; and each time I was shown another one, I would reply automatically, "Wait until Christmas."

Finally, all was ready, wrapped, and packed for the trip to North Carolina. The

closer we got to the mountains and grand-parents, the more excited the voices in the car became. The first glimpse of "home," as we drove up the winding drive, and the warm welcome that awaited us—along with homemade apple pie and a cozy fire—all added to our excitement.

This excitement, and the anticipation of all that was yet to come, built to a crescendo on Christmas Eve, as each child (and adult) hung his or her stocking in front of the large fireplace. My daddy gathered all the children around and called Santa, at the North Pole—just to make sure he had received all the lists and everything was in order—then wished him a good and speedy trip. Just as the children were all being hurried off to bed, Santa's sleigh bells could be heard above the roof. (They were donkey's bells hung on the chimney and rung by my younger brother at the appropriate moment.) Needless to say, sleep didn't come easily to the children that night.

Christmas morning arrived, and every-one rushed down to the kitchen, dressed in their Sunday best. By tradition, no one is allowed into the living room until all have gathered and finished eating. The children tried to be patient, as the grown-ups slowly drank their coffee and munched their rolls. Just as the last drop of coffee was being downed, my daddy decided it would be better to read the Christmas story before the stockings, instead of later. Amid sighs, he began to read the beautiful story. Even though the children listened, I am afraid they didn't hear much that morning.

Then, to make matters worse, my sister decided pictures should be taken as each child entered the living room, so the children were told to line up and enter one by one. This did it. My eldest son looked up at his grandmother and said, in total disgust and exasperation, "Bethlehem was never as miserable as this!"

Christmas Cheer
LOY C. GUY

We tramp through the woodland
And gather some pine;
Bring home the holly,
The best of its kind;

Spruce up the parlor,
Garland the door;
Snowflake the pinecones,
Two dozen or more;

Fling on the glitter,
Star-light the tree,
While Grandma relaxes
With hot spearmint tea;

Join in the laughter,
Grin ear to ear—
December and Christmas,
The best time of year!

BRUNCH FOR THE CHRISTMAS CELEBRATION

SOUTHERN SAUSAGE PINWHEELS

Preheat oven to 350°F. In a small bowl, sift together 2 cups all-purpose flour, ⅛ cup cornmeal, ⅛ cup granulated sugar, 1 tablespoon baking powder, and ¼ teaspoon salt. Add ⅓ cup vegetable oil and ⅓ cup milk; blend thoroughly. On a lightly floured surface, roll out to a 12- x 15-inch rectangle. Spread 1 pound uncooked hot or mild sausage on rolled-out dough. Starting on a long side, roll rectangle tightly into a log. Chill about 3 hours and cut into ¼-inch slices. Arrange on a greased baking sheet and bake 15 to 20 minutes. Serve with grape jelly. Makes 5 dozen pinwheels.

POTATO AND RED-PEPPER FRITATTA

Preheat oven to 400°F. Thinly slice ½ medium onion. Remove the stem, ribs, and seeds of 1 red bell pepper, and cut into thin slices. In an 8-inch ovenproof nonstick skillet, heat 1 teaspoon olive oil over medium heat. Add onion and bell pepper to skillet and sauté, stirring occasionally, until onion is lightly browned, about 5 minutes. Transfer to a bowl and set aside. Heat 2 teaspoons olive oil in skillet. Add 2 peeled, thinly sliced russet potatoes; season generously with salt and pepper. Sauté over medium heat, turning often with spatula, until potatoes are tender and lightly browned, about 10 minutes. Remove from heat and transfer potatoes to bowl with onion mixture; toss to combine. Return mixture to skillet and flatten with a metal spatula. In a large bowl, beat 8 large eggs with 2 teaspoons chopped fresh rosemary, ½ teaspoon salt, and ⅛ teaspoon pepper. Pour over potato mixture; tilt pan to distribute evenly. Bake until set, 15 to 20 minutes. Cut into wedges and serve. Makes 6 servings.

HOLIDAY AMBROSIA

Peel and core 1 large pineapple; cut into large chunks. Peel 6 large navel oranges and remove seeds; slice thinly. In a large glass serving bowl, layer pineapple, oranges, 1 cup grated coconut, and ¼ cup red and green maraschino cherries. In a small bowl, combine 1 cup pineapple yogurt and ½ cup grated coconut. Spoon over fruit and chill for at least 4 hours. Makes 8 servings.

*O*utside the window, snowflakes fall gently to the ground. Excited greetings and joyous peals of laughter rise and join the sound of the carols from the piano. In the dining room, silver bowls and platters, laden with the morning's meal, welcome the family to the sideboard.

The Waits

MARGARET DELAND

At the break of Christmas Day,
Through the frosty starlight ringing,
Faint and sweet and far away,
Comes the sound of children, singing,
Chanting, singing,
    "Cease to mourn,
    For Christ is born,
    Peace and joy to all men bringing!"

Careless that the chill winds blow,
Growing stronger, sweeter, clearer,
Noiseless footfalls in the snow
Bring the happy voices nearer;
Hear them singing,
    "Winter's drear,
    But Christ is here,
    Mirth and gladness with Him bringing!"

"Merry Christmas!" hear them say,
As the east is growing lighter;
"May the joy of Christmas Day
 Make your whole year gladder, brighter!"
Join their singing,
    "To each home
    Our Christ has come
    All Love's treasures with Him bringing!"

A Day of Joy and Celebration

Whatever else be lost among the years,
Let us keep Christmas still a shining thing:
Whatever doubts assail us, or what fears,
Let us hold close one day, remembering
Its poignant meaning for the hearts of men.
Let us get back our childlike faith again.
—GRACE NOLL CROWELL

GLAD CHRISTMAS COMES, and every hearth
Makes room to give him welcome now.
—JOHN CLARE

HAPPY, HAPPY CHRISTMAS, that can win us back to the delusions
of our childish days, recall to the old man the pleasures of his youth,
and transport the traveler back to his own fireside and quiet home!
—CHARLES DICKENS

Christmas is not in tinsel and lights and outward show.
The secret lies in an inner glow.
It's lighting a fire inside the heart—
Good will and joy a vital part.
It's higher thought and a greater plan.
It's glorious dream in the soul of man.
—WILFRED A. PETERSON

A man might then behold
At Christmas, in each hall,
Good fires to curb the cold,
And meat for great and small.
—THOMAS HOOD

Sound over all waters, reach from all lands,
The chorus of voices, the clasping of hands;
Sing hymns that were sung by the stars of the morn,
Sing songs of the angel when Jesus was born!
With glad jubilations,
Bring hope to the nations!

—JOHN GREENLEAF WHITTIER

Lordlings, listen to our lay—
We have come from far away
To seek Christmas;
In this mansion we are told
He His yearly feast doth hold:
'Tis today!
May joy come from God above
To all those who Christmas love.

—OLD CAROL

Heap on more wood!—
The wind is chill;
But let it whistle as it will,
We'll keep our Christmas merry still.

—SIR WALTER SCOTT

ONCE IN THE year and only once, the whole world stands still to celebrate the advent of a life. Only Jesus claims this worldwide, undying remembrance.

—AUTHOR UNKNOWN

Then let us sing amid our cheer,
Old Christmas comes but once a year.

—THOMAS MILLER

IT ISN'T SO much what's on the table that matters, as what's on the chairs.

—W. S. GILBERT

THE SPIRIT OF THE CRÉCHE

Pamela Kennedy

I decided that for once in our lives we would have a "perfect" Christmas. I would plan and prepare so we would eliminate that last-minute chaos so typical of the holiday. We would have bountiful evergreens and sweet, spicy baked goods and evenings by the fire with Christmas carols playing in the background. So I diligently set about to make it happen.

Things were going according to plan—until the weekend we were to get the tree. My son, daughter, and husband were busy, so I ended up at the tree lot alone trying to find the perfect tree. After hours of indecision, I chose a chubby fir. The verdict at

home that evening was not as enthusiastic as I had hoped.

"It will look perfect when it's decorated," I suggested. "You know what would be really lovely? Let's build a fire in the fireplace and play carols as we decorate the tree!" I offered. I located the Christmas tapes while my husband and son started building the fire. The music started, but something was terribly wrong. The Mormon Tabernacle Choir sounded like it was on tranquilizers as "Joy to the World" quivered from the speakers in a flat drawl.

"The heat last summer must have stretched the tapes or something," my husband said. I tried another tape, but the results were the same. "Maybe it's the player. Let's try them in the car and see if they sound the same."

We were sitting in the driveway listening to atonal carols when the children came dashing out of the house screaming, "Dad! Mom! Hurry, the fireplace is all smoky!"

We ran inside to the shriek of the smoke alarm as billows of smoke poured from the fireplace. "Open the flue!" shouted my husband as he fanned his way through the bluish air.

Later that night, after the children were in bed and the house was somewhat aired out, I sat going through a box of ornaments. I had the ominous feeling that Christmas was beginning to take on its usual chaotic nature. I was a week behind on my baking schedule, two boxes of unaddressed cards mocked me from the desk, and the number of shopping days left till Christmas was quickly diminishing.

In the bottom of the box I found the créche in a plastic bag. Clearing a place atop the coffee table, I began to arrange the pieces. As I stood the shepherds beside the stable door, my husband entered the room bearing two cups of coffee.

I smiled at him and patted the floor next to where I was sitting. Silently, we situated sheep and donkeys, wise men and angels. Looking at the quiet, peaceful expression on the ceramic Mary, I sighed wistfully.

"What was that all about?" he asked.

"Christmas," I answered. "I wanted it to be perfect and lovely and not all chaotic and confused and rushed this year, but crazy, unexpected things just keep happening and . . ." I looked at him with tears swimming in my eyes.

Thoughtfully, he picked up the figure of Joseph and turned him around. "I'll bet that's how he felt too," he said.

I was puzzled. "What?"

"Well, here he was all set to get married, then, wham! Mary hits him with the news that she's going to have the Son of God. And look at these guys." He picked up a shepherd in each hand. "There they were, having a nice, quiet night on the hillside when—'Halleluia in the Highest!'—tons of angels start shouting at them!"

I giggled at his dramatics.

"But let's not forget Mary here. She didn't even get to spend Christmas at home! I'd be willing to bet that wasn't in her plan!" He leaned over and pulled me toward him in a hug. "You know what?"

"What?"

"Christmas isn't so much about planning and schedules and organizing stuff as it is about welcoming the unexpected surprises of life."

We sat there for a long time that evening, and I still recall it as one of my favorite Christmas memories. I think of it each year when my plans get interrupted. I think of it when I begin to feel overwhelmed with all the holiday entertaining and I become discouraged about losing "the true meaning of Christmas." I especially think of it each time I tuck the baby Jesus in his ceramic crib. Because it is then I recall with gratitude how God interrupted the world one night almost two thousand years ago and changed all our plans forever.

Christmas Bells

AUTHOR UNKNOWN

There are sounds in the sky when the
   year grows old,
And the winds of the winter blow—
When night and the moon are clear and cold,
And the stars shine on the snow,
Or wild is the blast and the bitter sleet
That beats on the window pane;
But blessed on the frosty hills are the feet
Of the Christmas time again!
Chiming sweet when the night
   wind swells,
Blessed is the sound of the Christmas bells!

Merry Christmas

LOUISA MAY ALCOTT

In the rush of early morning,
When the red burns through the gray,
And the wintry world lies waiting
For the glory of the day,
Then we hear a fitful rustling
Just without, upon the stair,
See two small, white phantoms coming,
Catch the gleam of sunny hair.

Are they Christmas fairies stealing
Rows of little socks to fill?
Are they angels floating hither
With their message of goodwill?
What sweet spell are these elves weaving,
As like larks they chirp and sing?
Are these palms of peace from heaven
That these lovely spirits bring?

Rosy feet upon the threshold,
Eager faces peeping through,
With the first red ray of sunshine,
Chanting cherubs come in view;
Mistletoe and gleaming holly,
Symbols of a blessed day,
In their chubby hands they carry,
Streaming all along the way.

Well we know them, never weary
Of this innocent surprise;
Waiting, watching, listening always
With full hearts and tender eyes,
While our little household angels,
White and golden in the sun,
Greet us with the sweet old welcome—
"Merry Christmas, every one!"

CHAPTER SEVEN

The Joy of the Christ Child

For unto us a child is born, unto us a
son is given: and the government shall
be upon his shoulder: and his name
shall be called Wonderful, Counsellor,
The mighty God, The everlasting
Father, The Prince of Peace.

—ISAIAH 9:6

The Birth of Jesus

LUKE 2:8-20

And there were in the same country shepherds abiding in the field, keeping watch over their flock by night. And, lo, the angel of the Lord came upon them, and the glory of the Lord shone about them: and they were sore afraid.

And the angel said unto them, Fear not: for, behold, I bring you good tidings of great joy, which shall be to all people. For unto you is born this day in the city of David a Saviour, which is Christ the Lord.

And this shall be a sign unto you; Ye shall find the babe wrapped in swaddling clothes, lying in a manger. And suddenly there was with the angel a multitude of the heavenly host praising God, and saying, Glory to God in the highest, and on earth peace, good will toward men.

And it came to pass, as the angels were gone away from them into heaven, the shepherds said one to another, Let us now go even unto Bethlehem, and see this thing which is come to pass, which the Lord hath made known to us.

And they came with haste, and found Mary, and Joseph, and the babe lying in a manger. And when they had seen it, they made known abroad the saying which was told them concerning this child. And all they that heard it wondered at those things which were told them by the shepherds.

But Mary kept all these things, and pondered them in her heart. And the shepherds returned, glorifying and praising God for all the things that they had heard and seen, as it was told unto them.

TELL ME A
STORY OF CHRISTMAS

Bill Vaughan

"Tell me a story of Christmas," she said. The television mumbled faint inanities in the next room. From a few houses down the block came the sound of car doors slamming and guests being greeted with large cordiality.

Her father thought awhile. His mind went back over the interminable parade of Christmas books he had read at the bedside of his children.

"Well," he started tentatively,

"once upon a time, it was the week before Christmas, all little elves at the North Pole were sad. . . ."

"I'm tired of elves," she whispered. And he could tell she was tired, maybe almost as weary as he was himself after the last few feverish days.

"Okay," he said. "There was once, in a city not very far from here, the cutest wriggly little puppy you ever saw. The snow was falling, and this little puppy didn't have a home. As he walked along the streets, he saw a house that looked quite a bit like our house. And at the window—"

"Was a little girl who looked quite a bit like me," she said with a sigh. "I'm tired of puppies. I love Pinky, of course. I mean story puppies."

"Okay," he said. "No puppies. This narrows the field."

"What?"

"Nothing. I'll think of something. Oh, sure. There was a forest, way up in the north, farther even than where Uncle Ed lives. And all the trees were talking about how each one was going to be the grandest Christmas tree of all. One said, 'I'm going to be a Christmas tree too.' And all the trees laughed and laughed and said: 'A Christmas tree? You? Who would want you?'"

"No trees, Daddy," she said. "We have a tree at school and at Sunday school and at the supermarket and downstairs and a little one in my room. I am very tired of trees."

"You are very spoiled," he said.

"Hmmm," she replied. "Tell me a Christmas story."

"Let's see. All the reindeer up at the North Pole were looking forward to pulling Santa's sleigh. All but one, and he felt sad because—" He began with a jolly ring in his voice but quickly realized that this wasn't going to work either. His daughter didn't say anything; she just looked at him reproachfully.

"Tired of reindeer too?" he asked. "Frankly, so am I. How about Christmas on the farm when I was a little boy? Would you like to hear about how it was in the olden days, when my grandfather would heat up bricks and put them in the sleigh and we'd all go for a ride?"

"Yes, Daddy," she said obediently. "But not right now. Not tonight."

He was silent, thinking. His repertoire, he was afraid, was exhausted. She was quiet too. *Maybe*, he thought, *I'm home free. Maybe she has gone to sleep.*

"Daddy," she murmured. "Tell me a story of Christmas."

Then it was as though he could read the words, so firmly were they in his memory. Still holding her hand, he leaned back:

"And it came to pass in those days, that there went out a decree from Caesar Augustus, that all the world should be taxed. . . ."

Her hand tightened a bit in his, and he told her a story of Christmas.

There's a Song in the Air

Josiah G. Holland

Karl P. Harrington

There's a song in the air! There's a star in the sky! There's a mother's deep prayer and a ba-by's low cry! And the star rains its fire while the beau-ti-ful

sing, for the manger of   Bethlehem   cradles   a   King!

There's a tumult of joy
O'er the wonderful birth,
For the Virgin's sweet boy
Is the Lord of the earth.
Ay! the star rains its fire while the beautiful sing,
For the manger of Bethlehem cradles a King!

In the light of that star
Lie the ages impearled,
And that song from afar
Has swept over the world.
Ev'ry hearth is aflame, and the beautiful sing,
In the homes of the nations that Jesus is King!

We rejoice in the light,
And we echo the song
That comes down thro' the night
From the heavenly throng.
Ay! we shout to the lovely evangel they bring,
And we greet in His cradle our Savior and King!

Happy Shepherds
LADY LINDSAY

Happy shepherds, pipe and trill!
So your earth-tuned melody
Joins the angels' harmony
Far beyond yon snowbound hill.

Praise to God and peace on earth:
Christ is come of mortal birth.

Happy shepherds, kneel and pray!
First to you the message given,
First for you the song from heaven,
On that blessed Christmas Day.

Praise to God and peace on earth:
Christ is come of mortal birth.

Set in silver, as a gem,
Gleams among the stars yon star;
Ride the wise kings from afar
Toward the Babe in Bethlehem.

Praise to God and peace on earth:
Christ is come of mortal birth.

In a manger's grassy bed
He, the Lord of Life and Time,
Lord of each wide world and clime,
Meekly chose to lay His head.

Praise to God and peace on earth:
Christ is come of mortal birth.

The Shepherd's Dog
LESLIE NORRIS

Out on the windy hill
Under that sudden star
A blaze of radiant light
Frightened my master.

He got up, left our sheep,
Tramped over the moor.
And I, following,
Came to this open door.

Sidled in, settled down,
Head on my paws,

Glad to be here, away
From the wind's sharpness.

Such warmth is in this shed.
Such comfort from this Child.
That I forget my hard life.
Ignore the harsh world.

And see on my master's face
The same joy I possess,
The knowledge of peace,
True happiness.

THE JOY OF THE CHRIST CHILD

143

A Child Is Born

Jindra Capek

One cold, clear night, many years ago, when the earth lay frozen under a sky brilliant with stars, three strangely dressed figures could be seen struggling through deep snow.

Hoping to find shelter for the night, the men knocked on the door of a small cottage. It was opened by a shepherd boy, Josh, who cheerfully invited them in.

As they ate their simple meal,

and warmed themselves in front of the fire, Josh's visitors told him their story.

"We are three learned men—astronomers—come from afar. We are following a star that has proclaimed the birth of a child who is destined to change the world through love. War and hunger, injustice and fear, will be banished from the earth. There is no mistaking the star's meaning. Guided by it, we are journeying to salute the new king, long and difficult though the route may be."

Early next morning the three continued on their way, following the star.

Although Josh remained behind, he was deeply impressed by all that he had heard. A child would change the world! Could love really rule men's hearts? His head reeled with questions.

In no time he had made up his mind to follow the three strangers. "I too must greet this child," he decided. "The star will show me the way."

Accompanied by his little cat, Josh hurried to the village. He told of his meeting with the three Wise Men. As he spread the glad tidings, his joy made all the villagers happy too.

Forgetting their troubles, they started to sing and dance.

"Here, take this flute with you," one of the villagers said to Josh as he set off. "Playing it, you will gladden the hearts of all whom you meet, as well as the child's. Tell him about us, and of the faith we have in him."

The shepherd boy's route took him past a house far from anywhere. Outside, an old man was chopping wood, tired and out of breath. Josh offered to help him, and before long had cut enough wood to last the old man well into the spring.

Josh told the old man the reason for his journey, and about his hopes of finding the miraculous child.

"The winter is cold, and the road very long," the man said. "Take this woolen blanket with you to warm yourself and the child, and tell him about me."

So Josh continued his journey with his little cat, always following the star.

Eventually he met a small girl who was weeping. She had lost her way. Josh comforted her by playing his flute, and helped her to find her parents' house.

The girl's mother flung her arms around her daughter, clasping her tight. Once more Josh told the story of the three Wise Men, and the newborn child that would be the Savior of the world.

The woman gave him a loaf of freshly baked bread. "Take this bread and give it to the child," she said. "Tell him that we eagerly await his coming," and she wished Josh a safe journey.

Ever brighter shone the star, and at last Josh realized that he and his cat had come to the end of their journey.

Not everyone believed his story; some had laughed at him scornfully. Perhaps the Wise Men had been wrong about a new king being born. If so, what would he say on the

THE JOY OF CHRISTMAS

way home to the disappointed people he had met?

Then, in the distance, he caught sight of a dilapidated stable. The star, to his surprise, appeared to hover directly above it. Seeing the unearthly light shining forth, Josh's heart was filled with happiness.

As he looked through the stable door, Josh recognized the three Wise Men. They were gazing in adoration at a child held in his mother's arms. Tiptoeing forward, Josh gently wrapped the woolen blanket around both the mother and the baby to protect them from the cold. Then he took the loaf of bread and shared it will all who were there.

After bidding everyone farewell, Josh, followed by his cat, set off on the return journey. Walking along, he played so expressive a tune on his flute that those who heard it understood his message. It told of people's troubles; but it also told of great joy, and hope to come, for all mankind.

A Carol

A. J. ROBERTS

Of old, Wise Men to the manger came,
    Bearing their gifts, both precious and rare.
At the feet of an infant they laid them down
    As they breathed glad words of praise and prayer.
Of old, of old, in Bethlehem town
Wise Men and kings laid their offerings down.

Of old, the shepherds on Judea's plains,
    Watching their flocks in the cheerless night,
Saw in the east a great Star shine,
    And they left their watch to follow its light.
Of old, of old, how bright the Star
That guided the wondering shepherds afar!

Of old, the voices of angel choirs
    Sang the joy of a Savior's birth,
And the glory of God shone bright around
    As they chanted their message of "Peace on earth!"
Of old, great joy to the world was given
When Christ the Lord came down from heaven.

A Christmas Carol

JAMES RUSSELL LOWELL

"What means this glory round our feet,"
The Magi mused, "more bright than morn?"
And voices chanted clear and sweet,
"Today the Prince of Peace is born!"

"What means that star," the shepherds said
"That brightens through the rocky glen?"
And angels, answering overhead,
Sang, "Peace on earth, goodwill to men!"

'Tis eighteen hundred years and more
Since those sweet oracles were dumb.
We wait for Him, like them of yore.
Alas, He seems so slow to come!

But it was said in words of gold
No time or sorrow e'er shall dim
That little children might be bold
In perfect trust to come to Him.

All round about our feet shall shine
A light like that the Wise Men saw
If we our loving wills incline
To that sweet Life which is the law.

So shall we learn to understand
The simple faith of shepherds then
And, clasping kindly hand in hand,
Sing "Peace on earth, goodwill to men!"

And they who do their souls no wrong,
But keep at eve the faith of morn,
Shall daily hear the angel song,
"Today the Prince of Peace is born!"

The Wonder and Glory of His Birth

Some say that ever 'gainst that season comes,
Wherein our Savior's birth is celebrated,
The bird of dawning singeth all night long:
And then, they say, no spirit dare stir abroad,
The nights are wholesome, then no planets strike,
So hallow'd and so gracious is the time.
—WILLIAM SHAKESPEARE

'Tis Christmas night! The snow
   A flock unnumbered lies;
The old Judean stars aglow
   Keep watch within the skies.

An icy stillness holds
   The pulses of the night;
A deeper mystery enfolds
   The wondering Hosts of Light.
—JOHN BANNISTER TABB

Make me pure, Lord; Thou art holy;
Make me meek, Lord; Thou wert lowly;
Now beginning, and alway:
Now begin, on Christmas Day.
—GERARD MANLEY HOPKINS

PEACE ON EARTH will come to stay
when we live Christmas every day.
—HELEN STEINER RICE

We ring the bells on Christmas Day
   Oh, why?
      Oh, why?
To echo what the angels say
   On high!
      On high!
—ELSIE WILLIAMS CHANDLER

CHRISTMAS BEGAN IN the heart of God. It is complete

only when it reaches the heart of man.

—AUTHOR UNKNOWN

Smiles on thee, on me, on all;
Who became an infant small.
Infant smiles are his own smiles;
Heaven and earth to peace beguiles.

—WILLIAM BLAKE

All love and mystery in one little face,
All light and beauty in a single star
That rose among the shadows, pure and far,
Above an humble place;
All heaven in song upon a lonely hill,
Earth listening, fain and still.

—NANCY BYRD TURNER

No heralds with trumpets
the Prince to receive.
No welcome by cannon that
first Christmas Eve.
Just Joseph and Mary, with
straw for her bed;
A Babe in a manger, a star
overhead.

—EDGAR GUEST

The Christ Child stood at Mary's knee,
His hair was like a crown,
And all the flowers looked up at Him,
And all the stars looked down.

—G. K. CHESTERTON

LET CHRISTMAS BE a bright and happy day; but let its brightness come from

the radiance of the star of Bethlehem and its happiness be found in Christ.

—H. G. DEN

TROUBLE AT THE INN

Dina Donohue

For years now, whenever Christmas pageants are talked about in a certain little town in the Midwest, someone is sure to mention the name of Wallace Purling.

Wally's performance in one annual production of the nativity play has slipped into the realm of legend. But the old-timers who were in the audience that night never tire of recalling exactly what happened.

Wally was nine that year and in the second grade, though he should have been in the fourth. Most people in town knew that he had difficulty in keeping up. He was big and clumsy, slow in movement and mind. Still, Wally was well liked by the other children in his class, all of whom were smaller than he, though the boys had trouble hiding their irritation when Wally would ask to play ball with them or any game, for that matter, in which winning was important.

Most often they'd find a way to keep him out, but Wally would hang around anyway—not sulking, just hoping. He was always a helpful boy, a willing and smiling one, and the natural protector of the underdog. If the older boys chased the younger ones away, it would always be Wally who'd say, "Can't they stay? They're no bother."

Wally fancied the idea of being a shepherd with a flute in the Christmas pageant that year, but the play's director, Miss Lumbard, assigned him to a more important role. After all, she reasoned, the Innkeeper did not have too many lines, and Wally's size would make his refusal of lodging to Joseph more forceful.

And so it happened that the usual large, partisan audience gathered for the town's yearly extravaganza of crooks and crèches, of beards, crowns, halos, and a whole stage full of squeaky voices. No one on stage or off was more caught up in the magic of the night than Wallace Purling. They said later that he stood in the wings and watched the performance with such fascination that from time to time Miss Lumbard had to make sure he didn't wander onstage before his cue.

Then the time came when Joseph appeared, slowly, tenderly guiding Mary to the door of the inn. Joseph knocked hard on the wooden door set into the painted backdrop. Wally the Innkeeper was there, waiting.

"What do you want?" Wally said, swinging the door open with a brusque gesture.

"We seek lodging."

"Seek it elsewhere." Wally looked straight ahead but spoke vigorously. "The inn is filled."

"Sir, we have asked everywhere in vain. We have traveled far and are very weary."

"There is no room in this inn for you." Wally looked properly stern.

"Please, good Innkeeper, this is my wife, Mary. She is heavy with child and needs a place to rest. Surely you must have some small corner for her. She is so tired."

Now, for the first time, the Innkeeper relaxed his stiff stance and looked down at Mary. With that, there was a long pause, long enough to make the audience a bit tense with embarrassment.

"No! Begone!" the prompter whispered from the wings.

"No!" Wally repeated automatically. "Begone!"

Joseph sadly placed his arm around Mary, and Mary laid her head upon her husband's shoulder, and the two of them started to move away. The Innkeeper did not return inside his inn, however. Wally stood there in the doorway, watching the forlorn couple. His mouth was open, his brow creased with concern, his eyes filling unmistakably with tears.

And suddenly this Christmas pageant became different from all others.

"Don't go, Joseph," Wally called out. "Bring Mary back." And Wallace Purling's face grew into a bright smile. "You can have my room."

Some people in town thought that the pageant had been ruined. Yet there were others—many, many others—who considered it the most Christmas of all Christmas pageants they had ever seen.

The Stableboy's Story

JEAN CONDER SOULE

"I have no room," the landlord said.
"No room for one guest more.
And you seek lodgings here for two?
Absurd!" He shut the door.

Sadly Joseph turned away
To face the gentle maid,
While tethered in the crowded yard, a
Weary donkey brayed.

"Come, Mary," Joseph spoke. "It
Seems They have no room at all."
Then suddenly a boy appeared.
"Good sir, there is a stall.

"Indeed it is a rough-hewn place
Not fit for noble feet.

But the stable, Sir, is clean and warm;
The hay is soft and sweet."

Mary nodded willingly.
"A stable will be fine.
I like the smell of fresh-cut straw;
I like the sheep and kine."

All his life a stableboy
Could happily relate
The story of a lonely pair
Who came within his gate,

And how, within a manger bed,
On hay as warm as fleece,
Nestled in his clean-swept barn,
There slept the Prince of Peace!

Carol of the Brown King

LANGSTON HUGHES

Of the three Wise Men
Who came to the King,
One was a brown man,
So they sing.

Of the three Wise Men
Who followed the Star,
One was a brown king
From afar.

They brought fine gifts
Of spices and gold

In jeweled boxes
Of beauty untold.

Unto His humble
Manger they came
And bowed their heads
In Jesus' name.

Three Wise Men,
One dark like me—
Part of His
Nativity.

THE JOY OF THE CHRIST CHILD

155

BAKED GOODIES
FOR CHRISTMAS DAY

THREE KINGS BREAD

Preheat oven to 350°F. In a medium bowl, sift together 2½ cups flour and 2 teaspoons baking powder. Set aside. In a large mixing bowl, cream 2 cups butter with 2 cups granulated sugar. Separate 6 eggs; set whites aside. Add egg yolks to butter mixture one at a time, beating after each addition. Gradually add flour mixture and ½ cup raisins, ½ cup golden raisins, and ½ cup dried cranberries, alternating flour and dried fruit, stirring well after each addition. Beat egg whites and fold into dough. Pour batter into greased 9- x 5-inch loaf pan; bake 45 minutes. Makes 1 loaf.

TREASURE-FILLED COFFEE RING

Preheat oven to 350°F. In a small bowl, combine ¾ cup granulated sugar, 1 tablespoon grated orange peel, and ¼ cup chopped pecans; set aside. Cut each of two 3-ounce packages cream cheese, softened, into 10 equal pieces, for a total of 20 pieces cream cheese. Separate each of two 10-ounce cans of refrigerated biscuits into 10 biscuits; separate each biscuit into 2 layers. Place 1 piece of cream cheese between the layers of each biscuit and seal edges. Pour ½ cup melted butter into a small bowl. Dip each filled biscuit in butter, then in the sugar-pecan mixture. Stand biscuits on edge, overlapping slightly, around a greased 12-cup fluted tube pan. Sprinkle remaining sugar-pecan mixture and drizzle remaining butter over biscuits. Bake 30 to 35 minutes or until golden brown. Cool in pan on a wire rack 1 minute; invert onto serving plate. Cool slightly and serve. Makes 10 servings.

GINGER-CHEESE MUFFINS

Preheat oven to 425°F. In a large mixing bowl, sift together 2 cups all-purpose flour, 1 tablespoon baking powder, ¼ teaspoon baking soda, ¼ teaspoon salt, and ¼ teaspoon ground ginger. Set aside. In a medium mixing bowl, beat 1 large egg. Whisk in ½ cup milk, ½ cup molasses, and ¼ cup vegetable oil. Make a well in the center of dry mixture and pour egg mixture into well, stirring just until moistened. Stir in ¾ cup shredded mild cheese. Place paper liners in muffin pans and spoon batter into liners, filling ⅔ full. Bake 10 minutes; remove from pans immediately. Makes 15 muffins.

On a table in the foyer stands a porcelain Nativity scene, decorated with tiny jewels. A light from behind the scene reveals the delicate figure of the Christ Child, flanked by the smiling re-creations of Mary and Joseph. While holiday pastries rise in the oven, the graceful notes of "O Holy Night" fill the house.

Child

ELIZABETH ROONEY

Dear child, sweet child,
Sleeping in the straw,
We who come to worship you
Kneel now in awe.

Dear child, sweet child,
Sheltered in a stable,
Each of us would bring you
Gifts, as we are able.

Dear child, sweet child,
Lighted by a star,
Help our hearts to find you
No matter where we are.

Dear child, sweet child,
Willing to be man,
Teach us how to love you.
No one else can.

Christmas Everywhere

PHILLIPS BROOKS

Everywhere, everywhere, Christmas tonight!
    Christmas in the lands of the fir tree and pine,
    Christmas in lands of the palm tree and vine,
    Christmas where snow peaks stand solemn and white,
    Christmas where cornfields stand sunny and bright,
Everywhere, everywhere, Christmas tonight!

    Christmas where children are hopeful and gay,
    Christmas where old men are patient and gray,
    Christmas where peace like a dove in his flight,
    Broods o'er brave men in the thick of the fight;
Everywhere, everywhere, Christmas tonight!

    For the Christ Child who comes is the Master of all;
    No palace too great and no cottage too small;
    The Angels who welcome Him sing from the height,
    "In the city of David a King in His might."
Everywhere, everywhere, Christmas tonight!

INDEX